Adventures
Abroad

adventures

THE STUDENT'S GUIDE TO STUDYING OVERSEAS
Stephen E. Loflin,
National Society of Collegiate Scholars

New York

This publication is designed to provide accurate and authoritative information in regard to the subject matter covered. It is sold with the understanding that the publisher is not engaged in rendering legal, accounting, or other professional service. If legal advice or other expert assistance is required, the services of a competent professional should be sought.

Editorial Director: Jennifer Farthing
Editors: Ruth Baygell and Sheryl Gordon
Production Editor: Fred Urfer
Typesetter: PBS & Associates
Production Designer: Ivelisse Robles Marrero
Cover Designer: Carly Schnur
Illustrator: Frank Montagna

© 2007 by the National Society of Collegiate Scholars

Published by Kaplan Publishing, a division of Kaplan, Inc.
1 Liberty Plaza
New York, NY 10006

All rights reserved. The text of this publication, or any part thereof, may not be reproduced in any manner whatsoever without written permission from the publisher.

Printed in the United States of America

September 2007
07 08 09 10 9 8 7 6 5 4 3 2 1

ISBN-13: 978-1-4277-5477-6

Kaplan Publishing books are available at special quantity discounts to use for sales promotions, employee premiums, or educational purposes. Please email our Special Sales Department to order or for more information at kaplanpublishing@kaplan.com, or write to Kaplan Publishing, 1 Liberty Plaza, 24th Floor, New York, NY 10006.

contents

Acknowledgments	vii
Introduction	ix
Chapter 1: Making the Decision to Study Abroad	1
Chapter 2: Preparing Logistically and Logically to Leave	19
Chapter 3: Gap Year Opportunities	43
Chapter 4: Adjusting to Your New Home	57
Chapter 5: Studying	85
Chapter 6: Exploring Your New Surroundings	107
Chapter 7: Gaining Experience	131
Chapter 8: Safety	149
Chapter 9: Being a U.S. Ambassador	163
Chapter 10: Returning Home	175
Chapter 11: More Postcards and Letters from Abroad	191
Appendix 1: General Advice for Family Members	197
Appendix 2: Resources for Planning an Adventure Abroad	205
Index	219

Acknowledgments

I am always impressed and inspired by the members who make The National Society of Collegiate Scholars (NSCS) such a remarkable organization. As a collegiate honor society, NSCS really works hard to create experiences and opportunities that will truly make a difference for our members. The really good idea to compile stories, anecdotes, advice and experiences that NSCS members have shared regarding their adventures abroad came from NSCS member Jordana Cole. The willingness of Jennifer Farthing and Ruth Baygell from Kaplan Publishing to make the idea a reality was amazing. NSCS staff member Andrea Cuba did an amazing job of coordinating surveys and corresponding with members. Thanks to Virginia Amos, Sara Boyer, Dalinda Dennis, LaToya Drake, Jim Duncan, Jennifer Fortney, Atiya Frederick, Melissa Green, Amanda Hapner, Shanna Houser, Ally Hudson, Bailey Kasten, Crystal Lemon, Betsy Lundgren, Rachel Piazza, Emily Rhineberger, Eric Samuels, Amy Shopkorn, Crystal Smith, Tom Smith, Erin Thomas, Caroline Warholic, Jennifer Watson, and the NSCS interns for the time and effort they have contributed to the success of NSCS and this project.

A tremendous thank you goes to Kim van Cleve. Kim was diligent, creative, fun and never overwhelmed by the prospect of organizing so many incredible ideas, stories, and advice from so many amazing NSCS members. Kim has tremendous experience working with students who are making plans to travel and explore abroad and her expertise and know-how was invaluable in getting this book organized and published.

The biggest thank you goes to the more than 600 NSCS members who have shared, contributed and participated in this project.

NSCS has a Scholar Abroad scholarship program to help make adventures abroad a reality for our members. Proceeds from this book will allow NSCS to provide more financial support for these experiences.

Stephen E. Loflin
Executive Director
The National Society of Collegiate Scholars

Introduction

WHO WE ARE

The National Society of Collegiate Scholars (NSCS) is the nation's premicre honor organization for first- and second-year college students. Membership, which is based on grade point average and class standing, is by invitation only. Our high-achieving students represent over 225 college campuses throughout the United States. Those who join NSCS have access to numerous opportunities, including scholarships, community service, career advice, networking, and study abroad experiences.

WHAT WE CAN OFFER

Because students affiliate with NSCS early in college, we have the unique advantage of participating in the majority of their college experience. Our early presence in students' lives allows them a greater opportunity to be engaged with other members. This interaction and the numerous member benefits differentiate NSCS as a meaningful organization; we work hard to be an important and significant part of our members' undergraduate experience.

NSCS also provides study abroad experiences and study abroad scholarships for members. The number of students choosing to study abroad has changed significantly since our organization was founded. It's no secret that we live in a more connected and global society, and the desire and capacity to experience other countries has taken off for high school students, college students, and young adults. In 2004, Congress established the Abraham Lincoln Study Abroad Fellowship Commission to recommend expanded opportunities for college students to study abroad, with special emphasis on studying in developing countries.

HOW TO USE THIS BOOK

This book has been designed to capture the imagination of the reader. The stories and advice compiled here, all from actual students, were written with the express purpose of helping others to think about how best to plan an adventure abroad. The students and young alumni who participated in this project are all members of NSCS who have recently returned from experiences abroad. They have contributed to this book because they are passionate about the value of spending time learning and exploring abroad.

We have collected the very best thoughts from our members to share—the tidbits they learned, discovered, and cherished while overseas. It may or may not be the best advice for you personally, but it should help you think about creating your own ideal plan and designing your experience. We hope that after using their knowledge as a resource, your experience will be easier because of things our members learned along the way. As you will see, the bulk of learning abroad takes place outside the classroom. True immersion happens when you leave the security of your family, friends, and all things familiar to see the world from another perspective. NSCS members unanimously shared that being abroad changed their lives.

Though every student has a vastly unique experience, we kept hearing one consistent theme: the impact of culture shock. Both upon arrival in a new host country and upon returning home, all students felt overwhelmed by the adjustment. This is normal and expected. The more prepared and open-minded you are about the experience, the easier you will find adjustment to the differences and changes. Be honest with yourself and the people you may be living or traveling with about any concerns or adjustment issues: Ask questions, seek advice, and approach typical things in atypical ways. In the end, your ability to stretch, adjust, and grow will make your time abroad life changing.

The stories that NSCS members have written and shared throughout the book provide a glimpse into the possibilities of being abroad. Remember, these stories are all opinions of the people who had their own unique experiences. You may find events that you want to relive exactly, or you may find pieces that you're curious about. The idea is for you to take away knowledge and inspiration so that when you do branch out on your own adventure abroad, you can make it the most memorable event possible.

As you read this book, keep the following in mind:

✈ Many sidebars, called "The Numbers," are scattered throughout the chapters. The Numbers are statistics resulting from surveys of NSCS students. You will find that the numbers don't always add up to 100 percent. This is because some NSCS members responded to all questions, while others responded only to questions that were particularly meaningful or relevant.

✈ The stories and information presented here are not facts. They are personal stories and opinions and are certainly not representative of all student experiences. Additionally, the information on social and academic customs in other countries around the world is merely the result of personal perceptions. Nothing written here is to be taken as an objective or judgmental statement about those countries and their educational systems.

Use this book as a resource to make your plans. Use this book as inspiration for all of the possibilities that are waiting to be discovered abroad. Use this book, and the advice and stories provided by members of the National Society of Collegiate Scholars, to start creating your adventures abroad.

We'd love to hear from you! Please visit us at nscs.org.

CHAPTER 1

Making the Decision to Study Abroad

"There are three important recommendations I would give a student who is considering studying abroad. The number one recommendation is to just do it! It'll be one of the most rewarding experiences of your life, and you won't regret it. Secondly, it is important to be open-minded and realize that you're the 'weird' one there—you're the outsider, the one who's different. If you go expecting changes, it'll make adjusting to a new culture so much easier. Thirdly, if you go to a country where they speak a foreign language, immerse yourself in that language. You'll learn so much faster and so much more if you only allow yourself to speak in that language and strive to not let yourself fall back to your native tongue. When I first arrived in Italy, I was struggling with even basic words, but by the time I left, was dreaming in Italian."

Tracy C.
Fairfield, Virginia
James Madison University

So you're thinking you are ready to go on an educational adventure to get to know the world firsthand. If you're like many students, you are full of questions about how to set yourself on the right path and make your study abroad experience one to write home about! NSCS member students had this same great idea and are ready to share their secrets to success, as well as the pitfalls they want to make sure you avoid. Going overseas for a year or semester can be the experience of a lifetime, but making smart predeparture decisions is key to a successful journey.

WHY STUDY ABROAD?

If you have picked up this book and have made the commitment to begin reading it, you are serious about the opportunities available to you. It's time, it seems, to stimulate your sense of learning in a whole new way—you're ready to take your studies and head for a foreign location.

But what has drawn you to the idea of study abroad? Is it the sense of adventure deep in your soul? The opportunities that studying abroad will bring you as an adult professional? Or just the knowledge that the experience will make you grow as a person? We asked students just like you this very same question after they returned from their time overseas, and here's what they had to say.

The majority of students replied that the *cultural appeal* of study abroad led them to this choice. But they went on to tell us much more about why they chose to travel overseas. With youth comes a questing to understand the people and ideas around you. And since the dawn of travel, education has been enriched by exchanges of ideas across borders.

2 ✿ Adventures Abroad

The Numbers

Reasons for studying abroad?

Culture	39%
Language Proficiency	24%
College Requirement	2%

With this in mind, students decided to travel abroad to quench their thirst for adventure, exploration, personal challenges, and, of course, fun! As a student, it is up to you to learn multiple perspectives on a given issue, and there is no better way to do this than by hearing and understanding these perspectives from the people themselves, in their natural habitats. And if you have a specific study goal, going abroad affords you the chance to have textbooks come to life in the form of architecture, art, language, history, culture, and music.

Going abroad is something many students felt compelled to do. They expressed a need—more than a choice—to experience another culture, with a "yearning" or love of adventure. One student stated that "God was compelling me to [study abroad]," while another student looked inward, discussing the challenge of "learning more about myself." What was clear to all students who responded, however, was that they had a reason for making this choice.

Even though this decision is personal, it does affect your entire family. Therefore, involving them in your decision is important. Your absence overseas would no doubt have an impact on them, and they must consider various factors about you going away. For the most part, the NSCS students consulted their parents but made the ultimate decision on their own. The majority agreed, however, that it was important to have family support.

Given the challenging nature of a study abroad program, experts in the field agree that having support is a key element to success, and in fact, research supports that fact. Students who were pressured into traveling overseas, as well as those who didn't have much support from home, were ultimately less successful in completing their programs. In other words, going overseas must be your decision, but it helps to have your loved ones' support to keep you there if you waver. That is the recipe for success.

WHERE SHOULD YOU GO?

The first and perhaps most fun question you have to ask yourself is, "Where in the world do I want to go?" If you have committed yourself to studying a language, your language interest might narrow the choices. If you have traveled personally with family or friends to a country that stole your heart, the answer might be emotionally motivated. If you have a specific budget in mind, you might think about which culture might best complement your pocketbook! Whatever the reason, country choice is perhaps your most important decision.

When looking at all the factors, NSCS students tended to rank language skills and comfort level high on their list. The factors of cost, safety, and climate were much less significant. (Naturally, those are important considerations, but they didn't seem to be the leading issues.) A much smaller yet still significant number of students picked their country based on the reputation of the institution abroad, the courses offered, and the caliber of the teaching.

"It is important to select a country in which you will feel comfortable—whether that means that you go into an English-speaking program, travel abroad with a close friend, or stay in a safe city. Also, try to find a program that provides other opportunities beyond just living in a city, like travel tours or host stays. This will help you get oriented in the world as well as in the city and country you are studying in."

Elayne Edmonson
Dallas, Texas
Texas Woman's University

5¢

Some logistically minded students picked their country for other reasons:

- ✈ Start and end dates of the program

- ✈ Exposure to other exchange students

- ✈ Specific program locations offered by their college or university

- ✈ Family living in the selected country (or originating there)

- ✈ Internship opportunities available

- ✈ Housing options (home stay, apartment, or dorm)

- ✈ Whether past years' students found the program fun and rewarding

- ✈ Ease of application

- ✈ Ability to transfer credits to home institution

- ✈ Culture of the country itself or the personal challenge living in this country would offer

- ✈ "Popularity" of the country, given the times and international climate

The Numbers

Main factors in country choice?

Location	50%
Cost	3%
Climate	2%
Safety	1%

Study abroad organizations would recommend that you focus less on location and more on the specific programs and what they have to offer. Typically, experts argue, a country's stereotype is often misleading and could send you to a country that is not what you envisioned. In fact, the Peace Corps and some of the larger and older high school student abroad organizations operate with this premise—they take the decision out of your hands and give more weight to your other goals, such as language skills and learning goals. Going on a program with no preconceived notions about the country is the best way to set the stage for an open-minded experience.

"Obviously, the factors that affect one's decision of where to study abroad will vary from person to person, but I think it's key to find some kind of personal connection with the potential country of your choice. I decided to call Tokyo, Japan, my new home for the spring semester of 2006 because my mother is Japanese, and I have many relatives that live in Japan. From this standpoint alone, it was a win-win situation! I could continue my studies abroad and have a chance to visit my family, which is especially rare.

My mother was supportive about the idea from the very beginning, which helped a lot, but other factors came into play, too. Something very personal and important to me was learning to get a better grasp of the Japanese language. My mother raised me to be bilingual, so I was fairly comfortable with my Japanese conversational skills. Reading and writing, on the other hand, were completely alien to me. I knew that studying abroad would give me the drive and desire to learn those aspects of the language, and by the halfway point of the semester, I had already grasped the basics. Not only did I accomplish a great personal goal, it made the experience of studying abroad much more fun towards the end."

Clarice T.
Corvallis, Oregon
Brigham Young University

Sample Destinations Chosen by NSCS Students

Argentina	England	New Zealand
Australia	Fiji	Northern Ireland
Austria	Finland	Panama
Bahamas	France	Peru
Barbados	Germany	Philippines
Belize	Ghana	Poland
Brazil	Greece	Russia
Canada	Guam	Scotland
Chile	Hong Kong	South Africa
China	Hungary	South Korea
Colombia	India	Spain
Costa Rica	Ireland	Sweden
Cuba	Israel	Switzerland
Cyprus	Italy	Tanzania
Czech Republic	Japan	Thailand
Denmark	Jordan	Turkey
Dominica	Luxembourg	Turks and Caicos Islands
Dominican Republic	Malta	Uruguay
Ecuador	Mexico	Vietnam
Egypt	Namibia	Wales
El Salvador	Netherlands	Multiple countries

"I finally came to a point in my life where I just wanted to do something on my own, so going to study alone in Sevilla, Spain, was easy for me. Over the last three and a half months, I have learned so much about life, but most importantly, I have learned how to depend upon myself."

Kendra Breucker
The Colony, Texas
Texas Tech University

5¢

WILL YOU GO IT ALONE?

Though the idea of studying abroad is a very personal one, it is not uncommon to want a partner in crime for your journey. As most personal travel is done with friends and family, should your study abroad experience be similar? Would it just be more fun? Our students weighed in on this question.

Perhaps the idea of traveling with another student popped into the heads of our NSCS students, but ultimately, they did decide to "go it alone." Whether it was a chance to make new friends going through a similar exchange student experience or a desire to have total control over their host culture experience, most NSCS students signed up for their programs alone.

Study abroad organizations support this idea. They would advise that you not make going with a friend a major factor in your decision. Just as living with a friend can be more challenging than you realize, revealing traits that you may not have seen before sharing the same space, traveling with a friend can be similarly jarring. Many organizations would report that students who have gone abroad with a friend usually end up branching off to make new friends or forging their own paths.

Making the Decision to Study Abroad ○ 11

SHOULD YOU TAP INTO YOUR HOME CAMPUS RESOURCES FOR ASSISTANCE?

Many resources are available to high school or college students seeking to study abroad, but these resources may be challenging to wade through. Studying abroad comes with *many* logistical questions, so asking anything and everything that's on your mind will help to get you on your way with fewer glitches. The world is changing every day, so changes with visa processing, credit requirements, living arrangements, etc. are par for the course. For the majority of NSCS students, the answers to these questions were sometimes best found within the walls of their own home campuses or high schools.

Students looked to the following people/places for advice:

✈ Study abroad office

✈ Trusted professors and advisors who alerted them to an opportunity

✈ Books, brochures, and study abroad fairs by the programs themselves

✈ Fellow students

✈ Online resources such as school websites

"It was always my dream to study abroad in Spain, but I am a nontraditional student and was not eligible to go abroad with an international program. I decided I would not let that stop me, so I applied for and was the first student from my university to receive a Gilman Scholarship, which helps American students pursue overseas study for college credit. I also received several other grants and scholarships from my university in order to embark on my dream, and I was successful—I was able to study independently in Spain for almost two years. While at first I felt inhibited without an international program, I feel like I was able to experience so much more than someone who has their entire program laid out for them."

James Ventin
Claymont, Delaware
Temple University

SHOULD YOU CHOOSE A HOME STAY?

Studying abroad means living abroad, and it is common knowledge that your home environment affects your learning success. Where to live (in a dorm/apartment or with a family) when you study overseas is a very important question. Regardless of the final outcome of your program—positive or negative—where you live will significantly impact your experience.

About 25 percent of NSCS students went abroad through programs that offered a choice in this matter. Of the 25 percent who could decide for themselves, around two-thirds decided on home stay. Ultimately, including those for whom it was mandatory, nearly 25 percent of all students lived with a host. Also, many programs offer students at least the opportunity to live with a family on the weekends, if not as a full-time option.

Those students who did participate in a home stay tended to be more vocal about the rewards of their experience abroad than those who lived in dorms. They believed their immersion in the culture was beneficial. However, those students who didn't live with a host family also reported making many native friends.

14 ☼ Adventures Abroad

Benefits of Home Stay

- You get to understand firsthand the perspective of the host culture and break stereotypes.
- You receive at-home help with language proficiency.
- You receive home-cooked meals.
- You live in a fully equipped house.
- Ideally, you can make lifelong friendships.
- You have built-in familial support to help with homesickness.
- You get a sense of community through the host family's social connections.
- You have personal tour guides to landmarks and hidden favorite spots.
- You pay less than you would in a dorm/apartment.
- You assimilate into culture more quickly through home living immersion.

Challenges of Home Stay

- You might get placed with a family who chooses to host only for financial reasons.
- You'll experience language barriers.
- You might have less independence than if you lived on your own.
- You might be used to the friendly, communal style of the university dorm living experience.
- You'll have to live by another family's rules.

"I was so nervous about doing a home stay in Madrid. Friends had told me how much they enjoyed living with a 'señora' and that I shouldn't worry, but I couldn't help it. I must say, however, it has turned out to be one of my favorite parts of living here in Spain. My señora, Geli, and her husband Luis live some distance from my university, but even so, I don't mind the commute knowing I have a real family to come home to.

Every day, they ask me what I've been up to, and I really feel like I am a part of their family, which means so much when I think about how far I am from my family in the United States. Even more, their 'nietos,' or grandchildren, are at the house several times a week, and they all treat me like another sibling. Nacho, the oldest, loves it when I play football or Frisbee with him. He's taking English in school, and we talk about expressions he can use in class. The second nieto, Daniella, loves to draw. Her smile and curly hair bob around the kitchen as she giggles with a pencil in her hand. The youngest is the two-year-old Nicolas, who chases after his older siblings. He also loves to color and will climb up on me, hoping for a piggyback ride. All of the grandchildren really make my home stay much more than a place to sleep, and I am somewhat envious of them because I never had the chance to visit my own grandparents.

My host sister (the daughter of my señora), Isabela, lives at home and has proven to be wonderful company and a valuable resource. She is always offering her help with any questions I have about the Spanish language or sights to see in Madrid. Her mother is a wonderful cook, and I am always pleasantly surprised to see my laundry folded and ironed (it would never happen at my home). Luis, my 'señor,' is quiet, but so friendly and caring—he came with me to my university on my first day to make sure I didn't get lost. The whole experience of living with a family has been so wonderful, and I'll certainly miss them all when I return to the United States in two weeks. The nietos are already starting to grab onto my legs and cry out, 'No te vayas a los Estados Unidos!' or, 'Don't go the United States!' As much as I miss my family in the United States, I know I will always have a family who really cares for me here in Madrid."

Russell Nemiroff
Yardley, Pennsylvania
The George Washington University

NSCS TAKE-ABROADS

✈ Consult with and include family in your decision-making process. Your family needs to be educated so they can be supportive.

✈ Country choice is a crucial decision—think long and hard about what you want out of your experience abroad before deciding on your destination.

✈ Tap into available resources, like on-campus study abroad offices and guidance counselors, when planning the details of your trip.

✈ Even great friends are not always the best travel companions.

✈ Even if you don't live with one, find a way to get to know a native family while abroad.

CHAPTER

2

Preparing Logistically and Logically to Leave

Before you leave for your big adventure, you'll need to get many logistics sorted out to ensure you stay connected (but not too connected!) to family and friends.

WHAT DOCUMENTATION AND PAPERWORK MUST BE PREPARED?

As you would expect, documentation needs to be prepared *before* you walk out the door—not only so you can get into your country of choice but also so you can head back home someday! Though the vast majority of students don't run into difficulties obtaining their passport or visas, some do. In those cases, the particular countries students selected had new visa regulations and policies. Visa processing around the world has changed in recent years, and you will need to know where to get the most up-to-date information. Given the complexities of visa policies, you can imagine that this is the perfect area to seek special assistance through your school's study abroad office. Many of our NSCS students did.

Students faced an assortment of challenges when gathering paperwork for overseas study. For many, the distance of the embassy from their home and its hours of operation (many visas require an in-person interview) were challenges. Other things you should anticipate are:

- A lengthy and complicated process that takes longer than you expect

- Dual citizenship issues

- Confusion within embassies themselves, given the recent changes to many policies

- Medical exams for an array of immunizations

- Issues with receiving documents on time at the right address

- Language barriers

- Passport picture issues

- Long lines or waits for appointments

- Overlooked details on letters or methods of payment

So what is the advice of students who have encountered these assorted challenges? Start the process *early*, they say, and seek assistance along the way. With all the planning needed and the time required for documents to reach certain offices, you don't want to be worried about these details when you will have so much else to do before leaving. Another piece of advice is to *make copies* of all paper documents sent. It could save time and headaches in the future if anything becomes lost or misplaced. You'll need to be patient yet persistent about getting responses from your country of choice. The processing takes a while, but if it is taking too long, you will need to follow up carefully. And finally, make sure you *follow the specific instructions* for filling out the paperwork; you want to be thorough the first time, so you don't have to go back and correct mistakes later when you're pressed for time.

"If you are interested in studying abroad but don't think it's possible for financial reasons, it is still worth your time to look into the program and find out information. I never dreamed that I would be able to study abroad, but by attending a short-term program that was only a month long, I was able to afford it.

Make sure everything is planned well before you leave, and try to find out as much information about the country and the culture as you can. Don't wait until the last minute to do anything. I would also recommend using a credit card for the trip instead of a debit card, because it is less of a hassle and also provides reassurance: If it is stolen, you can contact the company to have it cancelled and you won't be held liable for any charges. By using a credit card, you'll also never have to worry about the amount of money available in your checking account, and you'll still be able to withdraw money from ATM machines. Just make sure that your credit card is accepted in the country before you leave, and notify the credit card company, telling them where you will be traveling and what the dates will be."

Tracy C.
Fairfield, VA
James Madison Uiversity

HOW MIGHT YOU FUND YOUR TRIP?

As they say, "Where there's a will, there is a way." If you have always wanted to be an exchange student but haven't had the financial means to do so, you can make your dream a reality through many creative means. NSCS students found financial assistance mainly from their parents, along with personal savings, scholarships, and loans. The number of scholarships available for students in the United States to study overseas is surprising, and every year some funds go unused. College/university study abroad centers and high school guidance counselors can help you with research into merit-based and financial-based scholarships. Many merit-based scholarships look for individuals who are wellrounded with school and community involvement, in addition to having a solid academic background.

NSCS students also used birthdays and holidays to request funding from relatives (especially grandparents) and friends for their trips. Some took on extra summer jobs and worked more hours to save up for their tuition. Another factor to consider, however, is that your time overseas may actually save you money over studying for a year at your U.S. institution. Some programs actually come out to a cost savings if you factor in all expenses you'd have in your home country, such as car insurance, your meal plan, and dorm living expenses.

In general, the advice that students give about saving for the trip is the same as for many other aspects of your planning: the earlier the better! In general, at least a year in advance is a safe time to start. Make sure also to include spending money when you budget for the trip. The amount of spending money you'll need will vary greatly, depending on the duration of the program, the type of program, country choice, exchange rate, your choice of home stay or dorm living, and your general day-to-day spending patterns.

NSCS students also advise having an extra emergency fund for those just-in-case situations, so that you don't miss out on any special events that might come up (think elephant rides in Thailand or renting a villa for a weekend getaway in the Alps). All agree that having a budget and sticking to it will ensure that you are financially equipped for the duration of the journey. You don't want to run out of money halfway through.

WHAT HEALTH CONSIDERATIONS SHOULD YOU TAKE INTO ACCOUNT?

Prior to going on a trip for any length of time, you need to ascertain the state of your health and anticipate any changes that could occur while you are away. Most programs require a clean bill of health and forms filled out by your doctor prior to acceptance. Also, you'll most likely need a physical as well as immunizations. Many of our students used a travel doctor whose job is to help prepare you physically for your trip, and some did research to see current recommendations for traveling abroad given by such organizations as the Centers for Disease Control (www.cdc.gov/travel) or the U.S. Department of State (travel.state.gov).

The Numbers

Received extra immunizations for overseas travel?

Yes	28%
No	46%

✳ IMMUNIZATIONS

Immunizations and vaccinations are a part of living in—and sometimes even just traveling to—another environment. They are in place to protect you from being exposed to unfamiliar elements overseas and are sometimes mandatory, depending on where you're going. The most common requirements involve hepatitis (A and B), tetanus, and diphtheria. Many parts of the world have the threat of malaria, and our students sometimes needed immunizations against malaria, as well. As malaria and other immunizations require time to lapse between doses, make sure you begin them with enough time to have the medicine in your body prior to leaving.

Depending on your destination, you might be required to have as many as ten or more immunizations. If your program will be in a more remote location or if you will be working with any animals, you might need an even higher number of immunizations. Once you receive your clean bill of health—including the dates of your immunizations—make a copy of it and keep the document on you at all times, along with any important health insurance plan information, such as your group number and the plan's phone number.

Preparing Logistically and Logically to Leave ❂ 27

✳ MEDICATIONS

If you require any personal medications, such as allergy or asthma medication, bring enough medicine for the journey . . . and then a little more to be safe. Transporting these medications across borders may also have special requirements. Investigate the rules and regulations for your specific medications well in advance of travel. You will also want to know the words for your illnesses so that you can communicate your needs in your host country.

In addition to any chronic conditions you have, you'll want also to plan for less severe illnesses you could experience throughout your stay, such as motion or altitude sickness, gas, indigestion, cold/flu, cough, headaches, etc. A general first-aid kit can be helpful—keep in mind that many of the brands you're familiar with at home won't be available overseas. Include, too, any daily vitamins, adhesive bandages, etc.

✳ OTHER HEALTH CONSIDERATIONS

A visit to your dentist is also recommended before departure, with enough time for follow-up in case any issues arise. Also, make sure to have your eyes examined, and bring along an extra pair of glasses or contacts so that you don't miss seeing anything on your adventure! Remember also to pack favorite personal hygiene products from home, such as creams or soaps, if they contribute to your physical well-being.

"In Turkey, I had an allergic reaction to a local drink that turned out to have horse's milk in it—and my guide didn't know of my horse allergy! I took my allergy medicines and my inhaler along with a bunch of Benadryl and simply let my body recover from the shock. I was glad I had picked a university with a good hospital on campus . . ."

Kate S.
Madison, WI
University of Wisconsin—Madison

✳ STAYING HEALTHY WHEN ABROAD

To help stay healthy, NSCS students recommend always washing your hands before meals or using hand sanitizer. Also, refrigeration is different in other cultures. In the United States, we tend to refrigerate items that you'll find are not refrigerated abroad but are still safe to consume. Doctors will recommend that you drink plenty of purified water while traveling and avoid street vendor food. Trying new things does not mean that you need to finish everything on your plate if you are concerned that it will have repercussions for your health. Use your best judgment and start slowly with new foods. Once you're confident that your body can tolerate the spiciness or the distinctiveness of the preparation, you can become more adventurous.

Many students also found that with a change of lifestyle and diet, they put on extra pounds. Slight weight change in either direction is normal. Just be aware of your activity level and caloric intake to keep yourself healthy. Avoid using food or sleep to help with the effects of culture shock or adaptation; instead, treat these emotional issues with dialogue. (We'll talk more on the issues of adaptation in later chapters.) Studies have shown some students develop physical conditions, such as rashes or stomach ailments, that are associated with culture shock; again, this is common. Being an exchange student is a challenge for your physical, mental, and emotional states, but for the vast majority, the rewards far outweigh the pitfalls.

"When I got to Japan, I discovered that their national health insurance is offered to foreigners at very reasonable rates. I bought it immediately, in addition to my other plan. It was worth the extra cost to ensure that my insurance would be immediately recognized anywhere if I were to get sick. I was very lucky."

Heather H.
Hicksville, NY
State University of New York—Stony Brook

Living overseas means you will be exposed to things you may never before have experienced, from possible climate change to dietary adventures. That's part of the experience. At the same time, use your best judgment when faced with the "newness" of another culture. There are ways to decline an experience without offending someone's cultural norms, and you are certainly permitted to use this diplomacy at appropriate times. If you know of any food allergies or dietary restrictions that limit what you can eat, you'll need to ensure that accommodations can be made. And finally, making healthy lifestyle choices for yourself (including the use of alcohol) is your personal responsibility overseas just as it is at home.

WILL YOU NEED TRAVEL HEALTH INSURANCE?

To safeguard your health, you may want to have extra insurance while overseas. Most health insurance plans will cover you while you are overseas, but you'll need to double-check this. About half of all NSCS students purchased extra travel insurance; however, less than one percent ended up needing it. Some programs provide extra travel insurance in their tuition costs; you should explore this option prior to departure. Some students also advise bringing extra funds to cover the cost of any health conditions, as you may need to pay up front and be reimbursed later by your insurance carrier. You won't want to postpone treatment because of financial constraints!

The Numbers

Purchased traveler's insurance?

Yes*	39%
No	35%

Got sick abroad?

Yes	30%
No	45%

*Of those who did purchase it, fewer than one percent needed it.

Of those students who got sick while they were overseas, nearly one-third sought assistance from the medicines they had packed themselves or from the local pharmacist or doctor. Most illnesses weren't serious and could be cured with some rest and basic over-the-counter medications. For those that were more serious, many students used nonverbal signals to communicate their needs. In the hospitals of larger cities and countries, a translation service is often available. Other students who were challenged by the natural environment (such as one student who was bitten by a spider) found local remedies to help. These instances taught them more about the culture and non-Western or untraditional ways to approach illnesses.

HOW CAN YOU STAY CONNECTED TO
YOUR LOVED ONES AT HOME?

The vast majority of students were able to find ways to stay connected to their family and friends while abroad. Technological advances have greatly impacted the student studying overseas. Email and Internet services have greatly improved the cost and efficiency of this connection as well. Unlike old-fashioned letter writing, email can make communication instantaneous. And phone services have changed to match the global age and are now more efficient and affordable.

Here's how the NSCS students remained connected to home.

✳ EMAIL

Students recommended for anyone going overseas to pack a laptop if possible, as wireless Internet is available in most countries or at least at most colleges/universities. If that's not possible, the college/university you attend may have computers you can use. Also mentioned as cheap and easily accessible were 24-hour Internet cafes. Students found them in the tourist sections of town or in most youth hostels. Email tends to be the most economical form of communication if you have a lot of information to relay.

✳ INTERNATIONAL PHONE CARDS

Some students suggest purchasing phone cards at home before you leave, as they're cheaper and easier to use. Plus, family members can add minutes from the United States if needed. However, other students felt that local cards worked more efficiently. Ask your program about its recommendations based on the country you choose.

34 ✿ Adventures Abroad

✱ INTERNET PHONE SERVICE

Many students mention voice-over IP technology as a great and very cheap service. These are outgoing services only—people can call from their computers, but no calls can yet be received on the computer. Costs mentioned ranged from free to $0.02 a minute. (Skype was the service most commonly used and, at the time of this printing, was free to download.)

✱ LETTERS AND POSTCARDS

Students found letters and postcards to be a fun souvenir for loved ones or for themselves upon returning home. Some students mentioned this form of communication to be the most exciting for people to receive. However, some reported that their mail arrived after a program had ended, and the cost of stamps for overseas mail could sometimes be expensive compared to the other forms of communication.

✱ DIGITAL CAMERAS

Students used digital cameras to take, view, and send photos immediately via email. Many also uploaded photos onto online galleries, so their international experiences could be shared with loved ones back home in color, as they happened.

✳ FAMILY VISITS

Experts will tell you that family visits are best saved for when you can serve as personal tour guide, which means well after you have adjusted to your country and culture. A visit at the beginning of your stay isn't advisable for your adjustment, nor is a midyear visit for reasons of possible homesickness. Toward the end of the program is a good time; you will soon transition back to life at home, but you're still enmeshed in your environment abroad. If you are staying with a host family, you must seek permission; if the connection you have made with this host family is strong, bringing your family from home to meet them could be a wonderful—and complex—mix of emotions for everyone.

✳ WEBCAMS AND MICROPHONES

Many computers now have Webcams or microphones already installed, but some students found they needed to bring these separately if they wanted to stay in touch this way.

✳ SMALL SURPRISE GIFTS PRIOR TO DEPARTURE

Some students left small gifts or notes with others at home to be given later to family members. Those who did found these simple surprises to be sweet for the giver and receiver!

❋ CELL PHONES WITH INTERNATIONAL CALLING PLANS

Students who used cell phones with international calling plans bought these locally in many cases, with current rates mentioned at $0.10–$0.20 per minute. Some programs provide these for students to rent. Pay-as-you-go plans were popular. Some students used text messaging, if they had the option on their cell phones, to send a quick message to a loved one.

❋ INTERNET CHAT ROOMS, INSTANT MESSENGER, AND ONLINE
    BLOGGING

For those students connected to the Internet, many referred to chat rooms, instant messenger services, and online blogging (journaling) for sharing their stories as they happened with loved ones. Students cautioned about experiencing miscommunications through instant messaging, however. Without the tone of voice in a live conversation or the nonverbal body language of face-to-face communication, challenges sometimes arose.

HOW CAN YOU DEAL WITH HOMESICKNESS?

Technology these days makes it easy to stay connected to family and friends at home. The connection is often immediate, allowing people to share the highs and lows as they happen. The benefits of these technologies far outweigh the challenges, but be aware that the real-time connection can be an emotional roller coaster of culture shock, for those abroad and at home. This instant sharing from such a long distance can heighten anxieties for your loved ones, so be sensitive about your communication's impact.

Also, be aware that staying too closely connected might hinder your own adjustment to the culture you have committed to explore. Knowing how much, how often, and what to share with home is key to success. Your family will look to you for the best ways they can support you; if you use them as your sole source of support, you will not only worry them, you'll also lose out on new connections you could make in your local community.

You'll also want to be cognizant of the impact your communication has if you are staying with a host family. From the inconvenience (using the computer when others in the home might like to) to the message the behavior itself may send (the notion that you would rather talk with your family at home than with those who are in the same room as you), be aware of how your actions could be interpreted. Talk with your host family about your habits and needs and see if they're comfortable with them. It may be obvious to you that you have great interest in their lives, but it might not be to them. Explicitly stating your interest is an important part of adopting a host family and is largely your responsibility. Although you will need to have a connection to those at home at times, Tracy C. of James Madison University wisely notes, "The point of studying abroad is to experience a new culture, not to constantly be on the phone."

SHOULD YOU CONTACT YOUR SCHOOL OR HOST FAMILY BEFORE YOU DEPART?

When you travel overseas, you bring all the stereotypes you have of a given country and culture with you. You also bring your own cultural values and tend to judge the world with these as your base. Many are so deeply rooted that you may not be aware you have them. The sets of values and beliefs that make up the world's cultures differ greatly, and abroad you will surely be challenged by a differing set of values and beliefs. For this reason, overseas study is richly rewarding and, some would argue, the best education you can have. You can never have enough time to prepare yourself for this great adventure, but the earlier your expectations are aligned with reality, the better for everyone.

If you are staying with a host family, they, too, will have stereotypes and expectations of you beforehand. Email, call, or write to your family about your goals for the program and share your excitement about getting to know them. Keep in mind, many programs do not pay host families a large amount of money to have you in their home. They participate for the other benefits of the program, such as cross-cultural interactions.

Being overseas will challenge you with many unknowns, so you should get to know as much about your school program or internship as you can before you go. This knowledge will best prepare you for what lies ahead, letting you focus more time on the actual studies, language, and cultural learning.

"Before leaving, I thought I would never be homesick, but I was wrong. But after about two weekends of sitting around doing nothing but eating and complaining about being homesick, my American friends and I finally realized that we had been offered the opportunity of a lifetime to experience living in another country—and that we were not getting the most out of our opportunity.

From then on, I started to spend more time with the locals so I could focus on learning the language and on the things I really enjoyed about the country. I still get homesick once in a while, but I just remind myself why I'm here and try to get the most out of all of my experiences overseas."

Emily Marzullo
Highland, California
University of California—Riverside

NSCS TAKE-ABROADS

✈ Start documentation and paperwork planning early.

✈ There are many ways to fund your trip—be strategic and resourceful in exploring the many options available.

✈ Be very prepared before you go for a range of medical issues and situations.

✈ Find ways to stay connected to your friends and family while abroad, but don't lean too much on phone calls and emails—you might block yourself off from a full cultural immersion.

✈ Your success abroad is built upon knowing as much as you can before you go.

CHAPTER 3

Gap Year Opportunities

"I took a gap year before going to college, and all I can say is: Do it! Do it! Do it! There's no finish line in life; why is everyone in such a hurry?"

Allison N.
Starkville, Kentucky
Western Kentucky University

The concept of a "gap year" in the United States has just started to be an accepted, or at least a considered, concept. Europeans, among others, have been doing it for years. A gap year could be the most unusual, creative year of your life.

WHAT IS A GAP YEAR?

You may have friends who have taken a gap year, and you didn't realize there was a name for what they were doing. A gap year is a planned year that a student, or anyone, takes between academic opportunities. For students particularly, the gap year tends to be between high school and college or between college and graduate school or the first full-time job. The reality is that life is an experience, and more and more students are willing and eager to create their own life plan rather than following the traditional path that society has dictated.

Taking a gap year is much more common and more widely accepted in European nations and those that are more geographically remote, such as Australia and New Zealand. In the past, a gap year may have been considered an activity for someone who is lazy, or floundering, or who has a lack of life focus. Taking a year off seems counterproductive to most Americans. Time that is somewhat unaccounted for can, for many, seem to be a negative resume characteristic, or possibly a sign of a serious character flaw. In our culture, success is often defined by knowing clearly what you'll be doing next.

In reality, there should be opportunities for an experience that will help you *decide* what you want to do next. College is certainly a place to prepare for your future, but experiencing the world can help you prepare for your future as well. Often a gap year is time taken to "find yourself" through working, volunteering, or traveling—a means of learning about life in a nontraditional way. For some, the year helps them decide on a course of study; for others, it gives them an edge when they decide to enter the workforce.

Creating a gap year for yourself can be an incredible exercise in self-awareness. Traveling is a great way to get actual world experience before you continue on into your adult life. The opportunity to get away from your usual setting gives you a chance to be alone for much of the time and to self-reflect. The experience might end up modifying your seemingly "ideal" plan for your life. And if you have no plan, this may be the year of exploration that gives you some clarity.

If a student is very purposeful in planning, the gap year experience can be beneficial for launching a more successful future. Purposefulness is key, however, and being purposeful requires planning and good focus. The planning needs to start before you depart and must continue throughout the experience.

Here are some questions that may lead you to consider a gap year:

- ✈ *Do I really want to go to college?* If you have always been motivated or pushed toward attending college yet don't feel committed to the idea, a gap year could be helpful. Many students do decide to attend college after their gap year experience.

- ✈ *Am I ready for graduate school?* If you think you want to continue your education or if you're sure but just need a break from academics, a gap year can provide new inspiration and motivation.

- ✈ *Can my first job actually wait?* After graduating from college, you may want to take a year before you start down a career path. When you are approaching graduation, no question gets asked more than, "What are you going to do next?" As members of NSCS mentioned, you have your whole life ahead of you, and taking off a year will not set you back. Your experiences can also make you more interesting and marketable when compared to other job candidates.

- ✈ *What about a gap year between jobs?* Depending on your financial situation, taking a year off between jobs can be beneficial. Perhaps your career isn't where you want it to be, or you're out of a job and have limited prospects. The gap year could be the right time to make decisions about next steps. You may find yourself in a different place regarding financial support from family, so you need to be especially diligent about your financial plan, especially if you have debt or other obligations.

HOW CAN YOU MAKE THE MOST OF YOUR GAP YEAR?

Of the small number of NSCS students who took a gap year, half used the time to gain real work experience, and the other half traveled overseas. Some worked for the government, at a non-profit agency, or in business to prepare for academic classroom experience and/or the working world. Other students spent the year after their senior year learning a different language and culture as international exchange students. Most of these students made arrangements on their own, though some did opt for an international high school exchange organization that offered a gap-year program. All students who participated in this type of program recommend it. However, they ask you to keep these issues in mind:

✈ Apply concurrently for college/university. Consider your options and, if necessary and possible, simply defer any acceptances.

✈ If you're on a waiting list for any college, make sure the admissions office knows about your plan to take a gap year.

✈ Initially, do not plan to take more than one year off.

✈ Save as much money as you can if you work (including putting money into retirement funds—this money is not counted against you when determining financial aid eligibility).

✈ Remember that study/work/travel abroad is not for everyone and that you get out of the experience what you put in to it. Your experience should have purpose; don't just go "for fun."

✈ You don't necessarily have to go abroad. You don't have to leave the country to do something interesting with your life.

"I would highly recommend taking a gap year. But you should still apply to universities and, once accepted, defer your admission. I would suggest, for your gap year, any of the following: traveling, working, volunteering, teaching English abroad, or getting an internship. Whatever you do, though, you should have a plan, and I don't think you should take any more than one year. If possible, I also recommend saving as much money as you can during this year; it'll help out with spending money or tuition when you return to school."

Tom B.
Annapolis, Maryland
University of Maryland—Baltimore County

NSCS students experienced many benefits from a gap year: time to think if college was the right decision, time to gain perspective, a break from school "burn out," preparation for independent living, and an experience to open their minds before entering college/university. You, too, might consider this nontraditional path; if so, just remember to arm yourself with the benefits of taking a gap year when pitching the idea to your family and advisors. Some students expressed that taking a gap year initially made them feel as though they were disappointing their parents. If you stay focused on meticulous planning and the rewards that will come from the experience, however, you'll have more confidence in your decision and an easier time convincing your family that this is the right choice for you.

MAKING PLANS FOR A GAP YEAR

Making plans to be away for a gap year is no different than making plans to be abroad for any amount of time. Depending on when you choose to take the year, there will be details to resolve with college, graduate school, or employers. You need to be focused on all of the necessary paperwork, finding accommodations, and making sure you have your resources and medical plans resolved. Once you have the basics, you can start focusing on what you actually want to do for a year. Here are some steps to take when planning a well-thought-out experience.

✳ **SET CONCRETE GOALS**

What do you hope to accomplish, and how do you measure a successful year? Think thoroughly about your goals and plans before you pitch your idea to your parents. If you have a clear and specific plan, your parents may be more willing to accept the idea.

✳ **THINK ABOUT HOW YOU'LL PAY FOR IT**

Always be clear, confident, and armed with good reasoning with anyone you hope will help fund your experience. Parents may not immediately leap to support idea, so you need to reassure them about your plans. If you're planning to work while abroad, make sure you complete all the necessary paperwork and confirm that you understand the various rules that affect Americans working abroad. (You can get good information from the U.S. State Department.) If you choose to work, you can consider a multitude of possibilities.

✈ One good option is the opportunity to be an au pair (a domestic helper). This kind of work allows you to work within a family, get paid, and typically have a place to live. Many families are somewhat flexible with schedules and often allow the au pair to travel with them on holiday. There are agencies that will help you with placement.

✈ Many U.S. companies have offices abroad. You may want to check with a local company for which you'd like to work to get the name of a contact at its office overseas. These positions may be paid or unpaid, but getting your foot in the door can be the first step to a great opportunity.

✈ Beyond U.S. companies, check online international newspapers for local opportunities. See the resources at the end of this book for more ways to explore working and traveling options.

✳ **CONSIDER DOING COMMUNITY SERVICE**

Numerous resources are available to help you find the ideal and appropriate volunteer opportunity. The rewards of this kind of experience cannot be underestimated. There is no better way to get to know the needs and people of a country than through community service. Many U.S. agencies have a big presence abroad and need staff and volunteers.

✳ **IF YOU CHOOSE TO TRAVEL, OUTLINE WHAT YOU WANT TO SEE AND DO**

You may opt to have a local person show you the country from their point of view. Try scouting the local universities; tour guides you find there will be near your age and may have a different perspective on local life than a more professional tour guide. Of course, NSCS students also recommend buying travel guides and doing as much Internet research as possible before arriving. Write down what you would like to do, then have a local person advise you on the best way to carry out your ideas.

✳ **CONSULT AN ACADEMIC STUDY ABROAD OFFICE**

If you have been accepted to a college and have decided to defer, or if you live near a college, you may get some good location ideas and country information from the study abroad office there. You should also make it a point to provide updates and feedback to that office when you return. Your experience will be helpful to others thinking about a gap year or planning for a trip to your country before, during, or after college.

"A gap year is great, but don't waste the time you take off. Think of it this way: If a job interviewer asked you what you did with your gap year, would you have something worthwhile to say? Be sure you take that time to further your education and intellect in ways other than studying, not let it just be a year that you have to breeze over in a job interview."

Julia B.
San Francisco, California
University of California—Berkeley

✳ **SHARE YOUR EXPERIENCE WITH YOUR FRIENDS AND FAMILY**

Constant feedback provides reassurance that the year is a good experience and keeps you connected with life back at home. Consider creating a blog where you can share highlights, photos and videos, news, and updates. You can also search online for similar blogs for ideas and suggestions from other travelers before you depart.

The possibilities for what to do during a gap year are endless. NSCS students have mentioned how learning new languages can be the highlight of any abroad experience, including the gap year. There is no better way to learn a language than through immersion. Whether you are expecting it or not, the gap year can be a time to become a better speaker.

To get the most out of your gap year, you must get engaged with your surroundings. Make it a priority to meet people, immerse yourself in the culture, enjoy the food, and spend quality time thinking about your future.

NSCS TAKE-ABROADS

✈ Decide if work experience or travel is your priority for a gap year.

✈ Taking a gap year is an opportunity to explore and become more self-aware.

✈ A gap year is a perfect way to confirm or rethink professional interests.

✈ Many colleges and professional schools will defer acceptance for students to have a gap-year experience.

✈ Gap-year planning and logistics are no different than planning any experience or trip abroad—plan out most little details before you leave so you can fully enjoy your experience.

CHAPTER

4

Adjusting to Your New Home

"When I first met my host mother in Peru, she called me 'preciosa hija mia,' precious daughter of mine, and proceeded to cry while hugging me, already telling me how much she was going to miss me when I left. Such open and warm love for a stranger solidified my observation that Peruvians love without fear and value the family immensely."

Katie H.
Berkeley, California
University of Caliornia—Berkeley

There is no denying that living overseas in a drastically new environment can be difficult. But because the rewards are so great, it's worth facing the challenge.

WHAT COMMUNICATION BARRIERS WILL YOU EXPERIENCE?

Three major barriers affect communication when living overseas: the obvious language differences, the nonverbal elements of communication, and the cultural beliefs that underlie them both.

Most likely, you have primarily studied language in school with a book, and oral conversations were secondary. One of the challenges with learning a language is that textbook language is quite different from spoken language. Speed of speech, dialects, and word choice are some of the major hurdles when the written word comes to life in daily speech patterns. Depending on the area of the country you are in, you could be thrown by phrases you have never heard; these colloquialisms of everyday speech make up the language of a local community. Slang, spoken in the streets but not in the classroom, will be a new challenge.

For the most part, what you learned in your textbook was not the language spoken in everyday life. It's also possible that the language of your classroom isn't necessarily the same language of your host country. Mexicans, for instance, use many different Spanish words than Spaniards. Also, tonal languages tend to be tricky for students, as they're very different from nontonal English. Sentence construction, too, can differ a great deal across languages, forcing students to think about language in various ways.

Some NSCS students stated that they were embarrassed at times to use their new language but found that the more they practiced, the easier it became. Even practicing their language at restaurants helped them gain confidence. Many others practiced by listening

58 ✪ Adventures Abroad

to the radio and television in addition to live conversations. Try not to be hard on yourself; you will begin to develop more skills. Getting into deep conversations will surely take more time, as establishing a fuller vocabulary takes time, but learning new words will be fun. However, some students mentioned feeling as though they "lost" some of their personality given this loss of speech. Keeping a good mental attitude is key for success. And if a local speaker uses English to help you communicate, remember that the local is doing *you* a favor, and it should never be expected.

Experts say that many cultures communicate using relatively little spoken language and that up to 90 percent of all communication is unspoken, using things such as a tone, a hand gesture, or an eye roll. Nonverbal communication varies from country to country and even within countries. Students commonly find themselves reverting to sign language to get their major points across if language escapes them. As cultures in Asia are more nonverbal than those in the West, the students who traveled to those cultures found more nonverbal communications to translate. One student discussed the importance of understanding methods for bargaining in the marketplace, what to do when you are a guest, how to speak with your teachers as opposed to peers, and ways to give compliments or "face" to another.

The issue of "face" giving and receiving is very complex. Many books have been written on the concept of "face," mostly in Asian societies. Giving and receiving compliments is an art form, and there are many ways to offend without realizing it. Humility is seen as a virtue in some cultures, and since Americans are often stereotyped as being arrogant and aggressive, students traveling to these societies face an extra challenge. Depending on your role in a conversation with another, your nonverbal gestures will either give or take away "face" from the person with whom you are communicating. Different words are used, for example, when speaking to a male versus a female, to friends versus a professional colleague, or to an elder versus a young child. The placement of your hands, eyes, and general body language might also "speak" for you without your saying anything verbally.

If you stay with a host family, you may find that you are at the same language level as the children of the home. They may even become the tutors who help you the most with your language learning. And even if you end up living in an English-speaking country, many students find that they end up learning a foreign language after all! As in American English, some questions are used in greetings but aren't meant to be answered, such as "How are you?" If you answer with a long drawn-out truth, you might be laughed at or thought a bit odd.

Many travelers find that English is indeed the "universal language," and even in the most remote locations, finding someone to help translate when in need isn't too hard. Students noted, however, that the English level varied from generation to generation. Most of the younger population had a basic knowledge, while many in the older population had not been exposed to English. However, in general, the more remote the area, the less English is spoken by all generations.

"One day, I was watching TV with my 'great-grandmother' at my home stay in Seville, Spain, and she began to tell me about Argentina, where she was born and had lived most of her life, and how she used to be a piano teacher. We talked for a long time, and I could tell she was happy to just talk to someone. It was then when I realized that in the pursuit of my initial goals of immersing myself in the culture of another country, my trip abroad had deeply enriched my capability to communicate and interact with others in another language. This is extremely important to me, because I plan to be a social worker.

My experiences will only help me to be more effective when reaching out to people in the future, and possessing the ability to speak Spanish will allow me to help many more."

Katherine Ely
St. Charles, Indiana
Indiana University

"One of my goals over the next two months is to become much more fluent in Spanish, because I want to be a doctor in a Spanish-speaking country. I have to admit, my first week here in Argentina has been a bit frustrating, but I've already learned that despite the language barriers that may exist between two people, it is still possible to communicate in some way—all it takes is a willingness to learn, a respect for the new language and people, and a bit of effort."

Mindy L.
Athens, Georgia
The University of Georgia

Here are some tips on how to succeed in a country that has a language other than your own:

→ Presumably, you will have studied the language of your chosen country before you travel abroad. Once you get there, watching television and listening to the radio is a relaxing way to get exposure to verbal language. Students use online translator tools (such as AltaVista's Babel Fish) to help with their written communication. For some NSCS students, meeting a native friend or a fellow student from home who speaks both languages at an advanced level can help bridge the language barrier.

→ Don't be afraid to break out your dictionary.

→ Don't be shy about asking people to repeat what they have said or to slow down.

NSCS students had many stories, both funny and slightly scary, with regard to miscommunications. Some students found that if they encountered difficulties, it was hard to communicate to law enforcement. (When strong emotions come into the mix, it is sometimes especially hard to focus in another language.) Other students found that they ordered meals they would never have selected merely based on their mispronunciation of words. Traveling within the country also became tricky in terms of language. Some students found deciphering train schedules and adhering to conductor requests surprisingly complex. At times, students admitted that they pretended to know what was going on but didn't. They noted that this approach usually led to confusion later.

Although living overseas and using another language every day can be exhausting, languages are learned much more quickly through immersion than in a classroom setting. NSCS students who received the compliment that they "spoke like a native" found this to be one of the most rewarding benefits of overseas living.

"Traditional Czech cuisine is typically washed down with beer, and although the food is, well, 'hearty' would be putting it gently, there usually isn't all that much of it (although some portions I've seen have been pretty big). That, combined with the necessity of walking everywhere, or at the very least of making one's way by public transport, keeps the majority of the population fairly thin. Well, that and their chain-smoking. Salads? They exist but are meant as starters and rarely taken seriously, unless the restaurant is catering to the tourist set. In general, the *bezmasovo jidla* (meatless dishes) consist of things like *smazeny syr* (fried cheese), *smazeny brambory* (fried potatoes), *smazeny* . . . well, you get the idea. Basically, most things come fried.

On the other hand, there is a somewhat healthy side to parts of the Czech diet. For one thing, there is the Czech passion for yogurt. It's really hard to overstate this: every little grocery, no matter how small, will have several varieties of yogurt and yogurt drinks. The real supermarkets like Tesco and Albert have multiple, fully stocked refrigerated aisles—the yogurt section is easily bigger than all other dairy products combined. Multiple flavors, colors, fruits, levels of bacterial culture infusion . . . a trip to a Prague supermarket would leave one with the impression that, in Czech society, yogurt plays a role somewhere between major export and deity.

There are many other dishes and products, both native and imported, that are commonplace throughout Prague—the goulash, my God, the goulash!—but I'll leave those for others to discover. The only other item that truly demands mentioning is the ubiquitous *rohlik*. Shaped like an enormous cigar and surprisingly flaky, the *rohlik* is guaranteed to be in every Czech home. At 3 crowns per *rohlik* (somewhere around 15 cents), it's one of the few truly egalitarian products of Czech communism—a baked good of the people, consumed by all the people! It has a cousin, whose name I cannot remember, made out of the exact same dough but shaped more like a Krispy Kreme filled donut. Under communism, there would apparently be shortages of one good or the other. It didn't really much matter, since they're identical except for the shape, but to this day, the Czechs who as children experienced *rohlik* shortages are convinced that *rohliks* are better, while those who grew up deprived of the alternately shaped variant insist that the opposite is true."

Dmitriy Zakharov
Mobile, AL
Georgetown University

WHAT ADJUSTMENTS WILL HELP YOU IMMERSE YOURSELF?

From the seemingly more simple adjustments, such as learning a bus schedule, to the more complex ones, such as being careful to not offend an elder, you will face adjustments throughout your entire program overseas. And many NSCS students are thankful for this.

✳ FOOD

Food is a large part of the human experience, regardless of culture. As such, it often becomes an aspect of living abroad that highlights the differences, but also the similarities, among people. From the time of day food was consumed, to the amount, to how and what was consumed, students noted food as something they had to adjust to quickly. Table manners also vary from culture to culture, and utensils differ from chopsticks, to hands, to a knife and fork. Even how to hold these utensils differs.

"Riding the train in Cape Town, South Africa, is always an adventure. Despite being warned about taking the train, my roommate Casey and I have ventured upon it a few times, making sure to take precautions: We never carry anything with us except what is hidden in secret pockets, we only go during the day in a group of at least two, and we go third-class.

The train is possibly the best place in the world to people watch, simply because there is an odd assortment of people on various journeys, each caught up in their own little world. But on one particular trip as we were heading home, the train came to an unexpected stop at Plettenburg, only a couple of kilometers outside of Cape Town. There was a garbled announcement that we couldn't understand, and then everyone immediately stood up and got off the train. Completely confused, Casey and I followed, marching single file through the bush to a set of buses waiting in a secluded parking lot. As we boarded the buses, I managed to find out from a woman nearby that they were fixing the tracks and we would take the bus instead to Stellenbosch, which was our destination in Cape Town. There were still questions flooding my head: 'Will this cost money? How long will it take? Will we still make it to the train station?' But I kept these to myself, thankful that the woman at least told me what she did.

Once on the bus we began to relax. It was moving a lot faster, and the seating was luxurious compared to the train's broken plastic benches. Unfortunately, this was short-lived, as we were dropped off at the next train station. We had no idea where we were at this point, and when we boarded the train this time, it was much more crowded. We sat across from three people in the strangest mixed and matched clothing I have ever seen. We finally arrived in Stellenbosch just as the sun was beginning to set, and we stepped off the train as if we had been seasick sailors and had finally reached dry land. But as unpredictable and unusual as the Cape Town metro can be, it has always managed to get us home."

Rebekah Hartnett
Manhattan, KS
University of Kansas

✳ DAILY SCHEDULE

Some students found their change in daily schedule to be the most challenging adjustment. Many cultures eat dinner much later (8:00 PM to10:00 PM) and only eat a small snack, having partaken of a large meal at midday or from 2:00 PM to 4:00 PM. Others found that the food presented was so unfamiliar that it was frightening to consider eating it. Students, however, all agree that you should try everything and remain polite. Doing so is part of the cultural adjustment, and you may even discover a new favorite!

✳ SENSE OF TIME

The pace of life differs around the globe, and stereotypically, the United States tends to be a faster-paced, "do it" society. This has both benefits and challenges. NSCS students found that they had to slow down for the most part. Some surfed and sat on the beach more, while others sipped tea and talked about literature more. As an exchange student, you are constantly learning through cross-cultural interactions. Take time out to relax and soak it all in.

✳ GETTING AROUND

Getting around may also be a major adjustment. The United States is a vast nation geographically, so Americans are used to driving places. Some cultures walk more given the setup of the city or the mass transit available. Students often find themselves walking or biking more than they do at home. A major adjustment you might face is that public transportation is much more crowded than in your hometown. Also, figuring out public transportation schedules and methods of payment can be stressful at first, but once the unknown becomes known, it can be quite simple.

✳ ATTITUDE

Attitude makes a big difference in how well you will adjust. If you can "go with the flow," you'll surely experience less trauma and stress. If you take on the role of an attentive observer, you can learn a lot about a culture. This may not come naturally to you, but NSCS students say it does help you adapt to your new environment. Soaking in the atmosphere this way will also ensure that others won't see you as the stereotypical rude and pushy American. Always be respectful; as an exchange student, you are reliant on others for many things.

Being open-minded to new people, places, and things in your adopted country will help you see what you yourself value and why you value it. Most students were not truly able to see their own culture through the eyes of the host until almost a year into their programs. NSCS students reported trying many times to remind themselves that all things American were not better. Ethnocentric viewpoints (thinking your culture has the best way of doing things) can hinder your learning and ability to make new friends.

Adjusting to Your New Home ✪ 69

"In Kiev I was impressed that, despite the sardine-can atmosphere of the buses and smaller 'route shuttles,' riders diligently passed their fares up to the driver; some asked for change, which was just as faithfully passed back to them by the passengers in between. It basically operated on the honor system, and I have a hard time picturing anything like that working in many other cities I know. At one point during the weekend, when a teenager was discovered to be trying to ride for free, he was sternly lectured not only by the conductor but also by various riders. Whether this public shaming was a lasting deterrent, I don't know, but the example of social self-policing was quite interesting to observe."

Dmitriy Zakharov
Mobile, AL
Georgetown University

✳ PERSONAL INTERACTIONS

Other adjustments tend to involve clothing styles, the way you'll interact in public, and personal hygiene. You might also feel that you just don't "blend in" because you look different. Body language, too, can be different in each culture. Proximity for a comfortable conversation differs greatly: for example, Latin Americans in general stand closer than Asians. And finally, personal hygiene may have to be adjusted, perhaps showering only at night, bathing only once a week, or using cologne. Washing your favorite sweater might also be an adjustment overseas, as laundry schedules may not be what you are used to.

✳ PERSONALITY

Personality plays a major factor in living overseas. If you are naturally shy, you'll need to speak up more often. NSCS students had to force themselves to spend time with host country nationals, even if this made for a more challenging experience. Limiting the connection to home also helped students "get out there." If you're making new friends, you might not need to call your friends from home as often. As our students found, this helped them get more out of the experience.

Another adjustment you will need to make is to rely more on strangers. As you need to ask more questions, you will find answers from the people around you. NSCS students found that it was up to them to start conversations. People won't necessarily seek you out; you need to be the one to initiate. Becoming involved with the culture and the people was the biggest tip the NSCS students offered.

✳ **GENDER ROLES**

Gender role differences were also a major adjustment for some students. What it means to behave as a male or a female is, in part, cultural. Some students found that the way they chose to dress overseas was more conservative than at home. This helped to avoid unwanted attention from the opposite sex. Some students experienced machismo in certain countries. But students warn to be careful discussing this topic with locals, as it is touchy and tough to understand cross-culturally.

✳ **GENDER RELATIONS**

Gender roles and courting are also different overseas. Some female students reported that they were shocked by the aggressiveness of men in their host country. Whistling and being approached by a stranger at a bar were not expected.

Remember that actions you are unfamiliar with are cultural differences in most cases, but you will also need to be hyperaware to keep yourself safe from potential threats you might dismiss as "just the culture." Same-sex interactions are also potentially different than those at home. Students were surprised to find that same-sex friends would hold hands or kiss each other. Being physical does not necessarily translate to being sexual in another culture's behavioral norms.

72   ✪ Adventures Abroad

✳ ETIQUETTE AND CROSS-CULTURAL PERCEPTIONS

Learning the proper etiquette so as not to inadvertently to offend people in the host culture was also an adjustment for some students. Depending on your country, making sure to say good-bye when you leave a store or looking someone in the eye when you toast can mean a lot. Along the same lines, debunking stereotypes and preconceptions about a culture is one of the duties of an exchange student.

An issue linked to stereotyping is your wardrobe selection. Look around you and choose outfits accordingly. You might notice that those sweatshirts, baseball caps, and sneakers are nowhere around, and you might be better off leaving them in your closet. Then again, if you are ready to represent your country, wearing them might help distinguish you from the crowd.

NSCS students also mentioned having to adjust to the ways in which students their age viewed alcohol. Laws vary country to country, but in many places, a large part of the culture for college students involves going out to pubs. However, students found that the amount of alcohol consumed differed, and that having a beer and a conversation was more commonplace in their host culture as compared to several beers and a more party-like atmosphere at home.

✳ OTHER ADJUSTMENTS

Other adjustments can include:

- ✈ Getting used to the different currency

- ✈ Living in another person's home

- ✈ Driving on the other side of the road

- ✈ Discussing U.S. politics with non-Americans

- ✈ Learning about a new religion

- ✈ Drinking only bottled water

- ✈ Limiting sarcasm

- ✈ Forming new sleep patterns (siestas during the day)

- ✈ Figuring out tipping

- ✈ Greeting with a kiss

- ✈ Using only the right hand (the left is seen as unsanitary by some cultures)

- ✈ Letting go of the conveniences of home

ADVICE FOR A SMOOTH ADJUSTMENT

NSCS offered the following tips for adjusting to another culture:

- ✈ Limit your interactions with other students from the United States.

- ✈ Don't stress out because you don't know how to ask—careful, quiet observation can reveal a lot!

- ✈ Laugh at yourself.

- ✈ Let down your guard.

- ✈ Withhold judgment.

- ✈ Be open-minded.

- ✈ Be careful not to offend.

- ✈ Take advice from tour guides.

- ✈ Be outgoing.

- ✈ Get involved.

- ✈ Be polite.

- ✈ Learn outside the classroom as well as inside.

- ✈ Get lost and find your way back (but pack a map, just in case).

- ✈ When in Spain, do as the Spaniards do!

HOW CAN YOU MAKE HOST COUNTRY FRIENDS?

Most students who made host country national friends did so through organized clubs, such as sports or music groups, at their university/college overseas. NSCS students also found that they could meet locals who also sought these connections via the international student networking groups. Several programs have "intercambios," conversation groups that bring native country nationals together with exchange students so that the program can be enhanced by friendship. Of course, an enhanced understanding of the local language was a big perk for those who branched into the community to make friends.

Other ways students connect with host country nationals are by going on a program alone or leaving the group behind to go out into the country. In many cases, students made friends by striking up conversations in public places with strangers. Many others made true friends in their host family or with friends of their host family. If the program included study with host country natives, students found it easier to make friends with students in their classes. You can also make friends at restaurants and shops you frequent. NSCS students also found friendships through those who wanted to learn English, in their internship placements, or in their university dorm placements. However, most students admit that they tended to hang out with other U.S. students. Also, many universities have large numbers of international students who form a certain culture of their own.

You will want to be cautious when making friends overseas, just as you would at home. However, those students who did make host country connections, either through friendships or acquaintances, found their program enriched by this interaction.

76 ❂ Adventures Abroad

CAN BODY LANGUAGE CREATE BARRIERS TO SOCIAL INTERACTION?

Half of the NSCS students polled believed that body language affects social barriers. Behavioral differences across cultures were found in the acts of head shaking, hand gestures, proximity while speaking, smiling, kissing and hugging, and soliciting affections from the opposite sex.

✳ **PERSONAL PROXIMITY**

A major element of cross-cultural communication involves the use of personal space, "the rule of proximity." American students studying in Mexico, Italy, Chile, and even England reported that natives of those countries stood closer than they were accustomed to when speaking. This closeness of other cultures is seen as warmth, and they must perceive those from "far proximity" cultures as colder. If you back up from an individual who is standing very close to you, you are inadvertently insulting that person or saying that you do not want to engage in conversation. Also, do not be surprised to find someone bumping into you on mass transit. Even if it is a "far proximity" culture with one-on-one conversations, the distance in public places may be defined differently, and you may find yourself too close for comfort on the subway.

Kissing and hugging can also be awkward if you are a student. The idea of kissing someone that you have just met—even on the cheek—can be foreign, even disconcerting. Hugging habits, too, vary according to culture. You may find that this action is too friendly for your comfort level, but try to go with the flow.

✴ VOLUME

Volume of speech and the way in which you conduct yourself in public can also be different overseas. You may have heard of the "loud American" as a stereotype. Students who lived in Switzerland found this to be the case: The natives were much quieter than the touring students from the United States. Loudness is very off-putting to others. Traveling in larger groups also serves to intensify the volume. The burden is on you to represent your country with respect for the host country, and this includes humility and soft speech in public.

✴ SPEED OF LIFE

The pace of walking is also different from culture to culture and sometimes represents the values of the culture. In environments where things can be "done tomorrow," people tend to walk more slowly (Spain and Latin American countries were mentioned as examples). North Americans tend to walk quickly, which is interpreted as being very busy with somewhere to go. Because the American culture is stereotypically focused on "doing" more than "being," this speed of walking helps to "get things done."

✳ SMILING

Americans smile a lot, perhaps more than other cultures. In cross-cultural communications, this smiling without provocation is seen as "leaking" emotions. When you smile, you might not necessarily be showing that you are happy as much as showing that you are friendly or intend no harm. In other cultures, however, a smile could mean you're definitely interested in someone romantically or could make you appear less intelligent (France and Russia were mentioned as examples). Looking someone in the eyes directly could also imply a romantic advance (Ecuador, Japan, and Hungary were mentioned) or be considered aggressive in a country where humility is highly valued. Needless to say, miscommunicated body language is not advisable. NSCS students warn you to hold back on smiling at strangers to keep you safe and to avoid implying something that you are not intending.

✳ GESTURING

Hand gestures also vary by culture. For instance, the sign for peace as we know it isn't interpreted the same way in the United Kingdom (it's seen as an offensive gesture there). Other cultures (Italy, China) also are known for communicating with their hands more than in the United States. Other examples:

- ✈ A wave hello might not translate. Or it might be seen as asking someone to go away (this was experienced in Thailand).

- ✈ Foot positioning should be noted as well as hand gesturing. Revealing the bottom of a shoe at someone or pointing it at a religious figure is a sign of disrespect (also experienced in Thailand).

- ✈ Shaking the head back and forth might not mean anything. In many areas, this movement connotes active listening on the part of the listener in a conversation (common in India and many Asian countries).

- ✈ A nod of the head up accompanied by a clicking noise can mean no (Jordan).

✳ FORMALITY

The (in)formality factor also contributes to the stereotype that North Americans are overly friendly. In other parts of the world, students found people to act more reserved, well behaved, and seemingly refined (England, France). The locals seemed to stand with good posture, dress neatly, and present themselves quietly and with careful, slow movements. Try to be aware of this as you travel. To have your hands in your pockets during a conversation with your professor in Germany could be insulting without your knowledge.

Some advice with regard to body language:

➜ There are always people watching you, so be careful in public.

➜ The opposite sex may take away false impressions from your behavior.

➜ Observe behavior carefully.

➜ Ask your local friends questions about this topic, even if it's awkward to do so.

➜ Be especially aware of this advice if you enter the dating world overseas.

➜ Speak in a soft tone.

➜ Take up as little space as possible when sitting.

When does body language especially affect communication?

→ When getting a taxi

→ In the dating world

→ While talking with professors

→ On the dance floor

→ On mass transportation

Most students reported that the awkwardness of interpreting body language got better as they became used to their adopted country. Students became more aware of their own body language and that of others and could soon pick out their fellow countrymen in a crowd. By the end of most programs, students learned this new nonverbal language and found it came naturally. In fact, some even found it difficult to come back home and have to readjust. You might find that you, too, will miss cheek kissing when you return to the handshake.

NSCS TAKE-ABROADS

✈ Before you depart, try to meet people from the country you plan to visit for lessons and pointers.

✈ Immersion is key for overall exposure to a country's culture and customs.

✈ Making friends is an important and unique part of the emotional experience.

✈ Body language affects social barriers.

CHAPTER 5

Studying

"I took only two classes abroad: a sculpture class and an art history class covering the end of the gothic age through the Renaissance—perfect for study in Florence. Our sculpture studio was located in the heart of the city and was a great place to explore our own creative expression and experiences.

A local art historian was hired for our art history class, but we only spent two days in an actual classroom. The rest of the time, under the art historian's expert guidance, Florence's museums, chapels, and churches were our classroom. Learning suddenly became an interactive experience, and exploring and understanding the city and the Italian culture was every bit as important as any actual course work. It was one of the most amazing and wonderful experiences of my life."

Megan Loeswick
San Jose, California
Loyola Marymount University

If you're like the majority of NSCS students on an educational study abroad program, you won't have a lot of difficulty adjusting to your classroom experience. Students find that the classroom experience is similar to that of home, especially if your instructors are English-speaking professors from the United States.

HOW IS THE CLASSROOM EXPERIENCE ABROAD UNIQUE?

Naturally, there are a few differences in the overseas classroom experience: a new culture and oftentimes a new language, for starters. Then there's the adjustment to a new class schedule and format, different teaching styles, new people and personalities within your learning environment, and finally, new standards for academics.

Classes can be much longer than you're used to—some lasting up to four hours without breaks. Focusing for this amount of time can be a major adjustment. Also, you might attend only one long class per week, which may make carrying the continuity of your topic/assignment into the following week a challenge. Weekends are also fair game for class scheduling in some countries.

The classroom's physical environment might also be a new experience, whether it be a difference in room temperature, humidity level, or ventilation. If your feet are cold, you might be distracted from the task at hand in science class. If you are too hot and the humidity is high, you might find yourself dozing off. Dressing in layers can be helpful for these situations.

If a new language is involved, the speed of speech, accent, or formality of the diction could affect your absorption of the material; you might find that an entire course could pass with little meaning filtering through to you. It's imperative that you ask questions to understand fully all the details of your schoolwork, including vocabulary words specific to a subject, complex theories, and deadlines and guidelines for classwork. This can be intimidating if you aren't a native speaker. Being able to express your thoughts is far more difficult in another language, but the only way to overcome this obstacle is to practice.

Although you are studying overseas, you might find that you are placed in courses designed for the nonnative speaker and that you have the luxury of being with fellow exchange students. This kind of class tends to be a bit easier to understand, with more basic vocabulary and slower speech.

"My host institution abroad, Palacky University in Olomouc in the Czech Republic, had six individuals from my school back home, Michigan State University. During the semester, the Central European studies program also hosted students from other American universities, as well as the Netherlands, Belgium, Spain, Portugal, the United Kingdom, Germany, and France, along with students from the Czech Republic. The learning styles of so many individuals sparked remarkable conversations, which helped us all gain insight into the relations and foreign policy of the United States with these countries in the European Union.

We had amazing professors who knew their curriculums yet were relaxed in presenting them—whether it be in the classroom, park, or the local café. It made me and my fellow students realize that the pursuit of knowledge within political science does not need to seem so stuffy. And of course, the friendships and networks that were developed through this experience have been amazing. In a couple of weeks, a few of us, traveling from as far as Amsterdam, are meeting in Washington, D.C., for a little reunion. It was an interactive experience that will continue to grow as we all start our professional careers."

Paulina Poplawski
LaSalle, Ontario
Michigan State University

WHAT EXPECTATIONS WILL PROFESSORS HAVE?

Your experience overseas is much more than a classroom and a final grade. You will be learning outside the classroom and gaining insights to which you cannot ascribe a grade. But it is understandable that you'll want to enjoy academic success as well. You will find, as you do at home, that professors' expectations overseas depend on the culture and on individual personalities. Be sensitive to cultural differences in the general classroom setting of your host country; watch and ask questions of your individual professors to determine their unique expectations.

The two most apparent differences in your experience with overseas professors will be the expectations of your language skills (if you're in a non-English-speaking country) and the expectation that you understand the cultural differences in classroom style. As an exchange student, you might be treated differently than native students. Your extra effort in coming to the country and learning the language and culture is usually taken into consideration with final grades. Professors' expectations of your work might be hard to decipher when you study overseas.

Many factors contribute to this:

✈ The classroom experience is influenced by a country's culture. Some cultures value lectures with facts and figures, while other cultures appreciate the personal experiences of the students themselves and focus on sharing in small groups. In Japan, a student should not speak out during a lecture but quietly take notes instead. In Germany, on the other hand, you might be expected to debate your teacher.

✈ All professors have a different style of teaching, no matter where they reside. You might find that you are expected to debate subjects, listen to experts only, or have group projects more or less than you did at home. In Spain, for example, lectures with a focus on memorization of the main points are most common, with group discussion less paramount than in the United States.

✈ Roles and manners are unique to every country, such as the kind and amount of respect shown to professors. In Spain, it's inappropriate for students to eat, drink, slouch, or put their feet up in class, though we're told that those things are slightly more acceptable in Italy or some South American countries. In fact, NSCS students in Italy were taken aback when native students climbed over tables during class or even left periodically to talk on their cell phones.

✈ Cultural preferences can dictate the structure of a classroom. In Greece, you might be told of exams or assignments only as they come up and not at the start of the course. If you're a planner, the more casual style will require you to adjust. Similarly, pacing will come into play. In Belize, one student found the pace of learning to be much slower than that at home, though it gave him more time to absorb the material.

✈ Attendance doesn't carry the same weight everywhere. In Japan, attendance is highly emphasized. In Costa Rica, it can be more lax; students tell us that while head count was taken every day, professors asked if anyone wanted to leave before they began speaking. Talking with friends was allowed, as were long cigarette breaks. In Uruguay, it seemed acceptable for students to get notes online and not attend class.

✈ Foreign grading may be different. Grading scales vary, and a number or letter scale may go higher or lower than the traditional 1–100 or A–F scales we see at home.

✈ Your classroom may be filled with fellow international students, and consideration may be made for different learning styles and speeds. Perhaps the professor skims the subjects more lightly so as to allow students to speak more, as in Vietnam or in Jordan. Or perhaps there will be a main lecture with no discussion from students, as in France or Ireland.

Studying ✿ 91

Another adjustment might be the way in which you manage your time and your learning. Students told us they had more freedom with learning while abroad, and with that came the need for greater self-discipline. With respect to schoolwork, you may not be told what to do and when to do it. For the typical American student, accustomed to deadlines for homework and exams, this freedom might prove a challenge. If you are a procrastinator, you may find it especially tough to handle.

Here are some other issues you may encounter with respect to time management.

✳ READINGS AND STUDY TIME CAN VARY

In England, Germany, Spain, Scotland, and France, students had enormous freedom in choosing their sources. They were able to select the books of their choice from a reading list and were tested only once with a final paper or exam. Readings were commonly recommended, not mandated. Exams, however, would indicate whether reading was accomplished and absorbed. This type of learning is self-regulated without structured homework assignments.

✳ HOMEWORK DEADLINES CAN BE SHORT, PARAMETERS OPEN-ENDED

In New Zealand, students were often asked to write essays with virtually no guidelines from the professor about what he expected. Expectations were "open to interpretation."

✳ ESSAY QUESTIONS

Essay questions are more common abroad than multiple-choice or yes/no questions, especially in Europe. Because the multiple-choice question is so common in the U.S. educational system, this is something to which many American students have to adjust.

✳ PERSONALIZED ATTENTION

Personalized attention or advice tends to be less common overseas than at home. Some students found that when they were lost, it was difficult to seek assistance to get back on track. Professors were not readily available for one-on-one contact. In China, for instance, it is not typically appropriate to ask the instructor for assistance. Yet as one NSCS student there explains, the tougher a professor is on you, the more that teacher likes you. The idea is that the expectation from you is higher. It is not that your professors don't care about your in-class performance; it's that they see your role as a student is to study and research to further the points made in the classroom. In Ireland and in France, students saw their professors as strict—almost "angry"—at their students. In Costa Rica, on the other hand, professors can seem like athletic coaches, not ranking much higher than the students. Some NSCS students found professors in Italy to be very demanding but also very interesting and challenging.

Studying ✪ 93

✳ DISPUTING GRADES

The process for disputing grades might be unfamiliar to you. The systems overseas tend to be stricter than those of the United States—grading policies are much more on the side of the professors, with no room to negotiate a final grade. If you receive a failing grade in Mexico, for instance, you would not commonly dispute it. Along the same lines, the student-professor relationship is also more formal vis-à-vis grading: The relationship you have or don't have with your professor will have no bearing on your final grade in Italy. So even if you have used your personal charm to help get a more lenient grade at home, this won't be the case overseas. NSCS students found some of their professors appeared more formal and aloof than their seemingly more relaxed and friendly U.S. counterparts. Having said that, professors do take into account the hurdles you face as an exchange student and might adjust grades appropriately.

Here are some NSCS student observations of academics around the world: (Note: These are based on a small sampling of students at specific schools and are not representative of every country.)

94 ◯ **Adventures Abroad**

✈ *Argentina.* A lot of group discussions

✈ *Australia.* Easygoing style, but high expectations; no curve in grading system; classes more attuned to students' majors

✈ *Colombia.* Many research-based lectures

✈ *Cyprus.* Tough, with great focus on final results

✈ *Denmark, New Zealand.* Tough, with focus on critical-thinking skills

✈ *England.* Tough, with a lot of readings assigned and professors treating students as peers

✈ *France.* Tough, with no curve in grading system. Professors expect neatness and might openly criticize students.

✈ *Germany.* A high level of language fluency expected and high academic standards

✈ *Greece.* Informal, with professors treating students as friends

✈ *Hong Kong*. Tutoring expected to be sought if needed for language

✈ *Ireland*. Somewhat lenient, with less focus on attendance

✈ *Italy*. Tough, with thought-provoking instructors

✈ *Japan*. Easier, with more lectures and fewer texts; attendance expected; fewer essay-based questions; a focus on social connections more than studies

✈ *Mexico*. Somewhat lenient with grades and little contact with professors

✈ *The Netherlands*. Tough, with minimal guidance from professors

✈ *Peru, Chile, Ecuador*. More relaxed approach to education *Russia*. Tough, with small-group work

✈ *South Africa*. Less frequent use of computer systems; little contact with professors

✈ *Spain*. High academic standards with a lot of memorization and lectures

✈ *Switzerland*. Tough

Here are the hardest obstacles NSCS students faced with respect to learning overseas:

- ✈ Language

- ✈ Understanding teacher expectations

- ✈ Getting to class

- ✈ Paying attention for long stretches of time

- ✈ Remembering that this isn't a vacation

- ✈ Having a lot of course work in a little amount of time (12 weeks, versus 16 weeks at home)

- ✈ Understanding local accents

- ✈ Learning without air-conditioning

- ✈ Not having Internet access at all times

- ✈ Staying focused on studying when there was so much else to do

✈ Listening and taking notes at the same time in a foreign language

✈ Balancing schoolwork, travel, and fun

✈ Getting clarification of assignments

✈ Surviving the heat and humidity

✈ Pacing the workload without assignments along the way

✈ Not being told what to do and how to prioritize

✈ Having the grade be based on one or two exams/essays, not on assignments throughout

✈ Getting over a fear of speaking and getting the accent right in front of classmates

✈ Staying motivated even if the grades won't transfer to school back home

And finally, here is advice for minimizing these obstacles:

+ Don't take notes in English; take them in the new language you are learning.

+ Don't succumb to the temptation to slack off if you only have a paper or test at the end of the course.

+ Don't be nervous to speak up and ask! Plenty of people can answer your questions.

+ If your course work is fairly independent in nature, ask your professors to clarify expectations so you can stay on track from the beginning.

+ Don't be upset if you have to learn by first making mistakes.

+ Really commit to learning, and you'll be able to grasp the new language.

HOW WILL GRADING WORK?

Upon your return to your home institution, it's quite possible that some of your grades will be translated as pass/fail, not as letter grades. If you do receive a letter grade, don't take it at face value: It's very possible that your home and host institutions will collaborate on how the grade should translate. Check with your academic advisor. Some programs give credit only if you test up to a certain level; others give credit only for a lower level of course work even if you take higher-level courses overseas. Others still give credit for the sheer experience of study abroad without grades transferring to your total grade point average. If you have chosen an internship program, you may receive 12 credits for your involvement in the program alone.

Before you depart, clarify grading procedures so that you understand what you'll need to take overseas. If you'll need to repeat course work upon your return, you'll want to know that, too. However, even if your time overseas doesn't "count" on your transcript, keep in mind that students who received no credit transfer while overseas tell us they would still highly recommend the experience. Some even knew prior to departure that their credits wouldn't transfer, and they made the decision to go simply for the adventure.

You may find that you need to petition to have your grades or credits transfer. If you're traveling on a program that isn't preapproved by your home institution, you'll want to clarify the credit transfer policy before you go. Most importantly, make sure it is an accredited institution. Then, if you need to petition, you'll have a stronger leg to stand on. Be clear on your argument points. Many colleges/universities will give credits for independent research if not for the exact course work completed. Some institutions require merely that you show a final project or a syllabus upon your return.

It's also possible that only some of your credits will transfer. If there's a cap on the number of credits permissible for transfer into your major, be careful. If you have taken advanced placement courses in high school and have already transferred these, you might have already reached this limit. Also, credits might transfer for certain courses but might not count toward university/college requirements. You might be able to fulfill a minor in your newly acquired foreign language with those credits. Or you can fulfill a diversity or language course requirement at your home institution.

Receiving credit for your time abroad is not always a cut-and-dried process, so you'll want to begin these discussions with your academic advisor early on in your planning process. And be prepared to go through some bureaucracy: Some NSCS students found the process to be a struggle, with full confirmation of credit taking an entire year to process after their return.

HOW MUCH STUDY TIME WILL THERE BE?

As you might imagine, a lot of variables determine how much time you'll spend studying once you're abroad. Most NSCS students feel that one or two hours per day is a fair assessment. Assume you'll spend the same amount of time as you do at home with similar habits. Some programs, designed to be experientially based, have less rigorous academics.

If a language difference creates a barrier to your learning, you can take several steps:

The Numbers

Felt the difference in language created a barrier to learning?

Yes   19%

No   48%

✈ *Select courses that will be familiar to you.* If you select topics that would be challenging for you at home, they'll be that much more challenging in a foreign language.

✈ *Seek clarification with your professor.* Even if you have to go out of your way to become clear on assignment needs, do it. Don't allow embarrassment to stand in the way of learning. In fact, you'll find that many others have the same question. If you're unclear on a specific point, write down the question in the margin of your notebook so you can follow up after class.

✈ *Get a tutor.* Not only will getting a tutor help your language and learning skills, it's a great way to make friends with a local resident. You may even want to swap language skills, teaching your tutor English once your lesson is over.

✈ *Make friends in class.* Having a friend in class means having a study partner. Each of you can shed light on things the other might have missed.

✈ *Use a dictionary.* When a new word is introduced and repeated as an important element to a key concept, look it up right away. Take notes on the word's meaning and study it later so it becomes part of your lexicon.

✈ *Don't translate everything.* If you find yourself trying to understand every word, you'll miss what is said next. Aim to get comfortable with general comprehension. Don't get caught up with detail words; that will exhaust you. Let some of the words go in the beginning, as long as you grasp overall meaning.

✈ *Be patient with yourself.* As you must know, language acquisition is not an overnight process. Between unfamiliar accents and unrecognizable colloquialisms, the language might feel brand-new—even if you have studied it for years. Take frequent breaks and ask a lot of questions. And don't forget that language learning can be physically exhausting; get plenty of rest, taking naps when you can.

✈ *Consider changing the course in which you enrolled.* In some cases, you may be placed in a level of course work that is too challenging. Discuss this with your professor or advisor and, if needed, make an adjustment. Learning a new language should be a challenge, but it should be an appropriate challenge. However, if a professor's accent is giving you a hard time, you can overcome this with time.

NSCS TAKE-ABROADS

✈ Cultural differences will especially be highlighted in the classroom. Understanding norms for behavior in your host country will be paramount to your fitting in and being successful.

✈ Don't be afraid to participate in classroom discussions in your new language. Speaking out will help your confidence, your vocabulary, and perhaps your grade.

✈ Professors overseas might expect the same of you with regard to hard work and attendance as from their native students, but will understand that you are overseas for more than the classroom experience.

✈ Work with your home institution before leaving to ensure that you understand the credit transfer process for your chosen overseas program.

✈ There are many ways to overcome a language barrier, but the best way is consistently to ask clarification questions when in doubt.

CHAPTER

6

Exploring Your New Surroundings

"I traveled to Rome with six girls for a weekend, but I couldn't get a room at the same bed and breakfast where they were staying, so I got a room nearby. We agreed to meet at the Sistine Chapel the next morning, but they never showed up. I waited for a little while, but after an hour, I decided I couldn't wait for them any longer and went in by myself—I wasn't going to pass up an opportunity to see the Vatican.

After that, I spent the day exploring some of Rome's other sights and had dinner at a little restaurant that I discovered on the way. When I returned to my room that night, I got an apologetic phone call from the girls, who said that by the time they got to the Sistine Chapel, the line was too long. They then set out to see some of Rome's other landmarks but instead spent most of the day bickering about where they should go next and eventually split up.

After I got off the phone, I realized that I was happy the day turned out the way it did for me, and while it would have been nice (and safer) to have traveling companions that day, I had the benefit of being able to do exactly what I wanted to do, on my own time."

Paul Bragin
Evansville, Indiana
University of Evansville

Exploring is a wonderful part of your overseas adventure, whether it's finding your way home from class or hiking some ruins in a nearby country. Most students who travel abroad feel that getting around is easy and, with student discounts, inexpensive as well. Many NSCS students cite Europe's transit system, in particular, as superior to any means of getting around in the United States. Overwhelmingly, NSCS students recalled saying there was "too much to do, too little time."

There will be myriad things to do and places to see once you're abroad, so naturally, you'll have to decide how to decide!

What is your travel style? Do you want to see a few sites at a slower pace and be open to what the day brings? Do you want to see as many major landmarks as possible, if only for a short while? Either way, you should just know your own style in advance. You may not have another opportunity to visit these places. To see everything you want to see, you might want to consider arriving in your host country early or staying later, if this is an option.

Also, money is a consideration. Exploring your new country will undoubtedly cost money. Consider taking on a part-time job months before you leave so that you can set aside a fund for travel. You don't want to be in a position where you cannot afford to do some extra traveling while you're abroad. Exploring is a major part of the learning you will do while overseas.

Logistical realities will also play a role in how far you can explore. If you have only a day open, you'll have to stay close to your host home. Large crowds (during tourist season) might also impact your decision, as will accessibility to a given site. Expect to make compromises with yourself and with others with regard to making the tough final decisions on the locations you'll visit. Exploring, especially with friends, always involves give and take to make things work out.

108 ☼ Adventures Abroad

"Having been in Texas all my life, I was looking for something to spice up my life. I sure did find it studying in London! The city itself was amazing, but the fact that it was central to some of the most beautiful countries in the world brought about a whole new definition of experience within me. Every weekend abroad was an adventure, whether it was exploring the Lake District on the outskirts of the city or freezing on the top of the Eiffel Tower in Paris.

Within the first week of being in London, I had made friends who wanted to travel and have just as much fun as I did. We planned our first trip to Dublin, Ireland, and did all the shopping, sightseeing, and partying that we could squeeze into one weekend. Another adventurous weekend found us horseback riding in Wales for four straight hours in the rain, and yet another found us eating ice cream in the freezing cold on the Champs-Elysées. On our trip to Prague, we got lost for almost three hours on an unexpected adventure exploring the city. But just as the shopping and partying were incredible, so was being solemnly educated at the concentration camps in Berlin or at the Anne Frank Museum in Amsterdam. My weekend trips exploring Europe were definitely the highlight of studying abroad."

Mehreen Molidina
Dallas, Texas
University of Texas, Austin

If exploring is important to you, you will want to be prepared to stretch yourself and step outside of your comfort zone. Your open (or closed) mind affects exploring just as it affects language learning, cultural immersion, and all aspects of being an exchange student. Whether you are wandering your own host city or off on a weekend excursion, exploring takes time and patience. As time passes, you will not only become more familiar with the language and customs, but you will gain more confidence in yourself. Remember to be patient with yourself. Understand that soon you will be getting around like a native . . . or at least with less stress and confusion. Here are some tips for getting lost—and found again.

※ GETTING DIRECTIONS

Getting lost was a regular part of some students' experiences abroad, and asking for directions came with its own set of communication challenges. You will find some locals give directions that you might find hard to follow, leaving out important details that would be obvious to a local but less obvious to a foreigner.

As a foreigner, you may be judged as an outsider, and some locals may see your understandable confusion when exploring as an annoyance. This is just a matter of life overseas. Fitting in where and how you can is your responsibility as a guest of another country. Don't be afraid to ask for directions in your host country's language if you are lost. You will find that for the most part, people want to help you.

✳ CITY LAYOUTS

Most cities and towns in the United States were initially set up on a grid system, where streets run at right angles to each other. Many other cities in the world have a more circular design, which can make it tough to know where you are and where you are going if you are a foreigner. In place of numbered streets, be prepared for names. Because most students don't have the option of driving, you will learn these streets by foot or through using mass transit. At times, you may feel that the bus or taxi routes are taking you in circles when, indeed, a straight line is not an option to reach your destination.

✳ EXPLORING ALONE VERSUS IN A GROUP

Exploring alone has some benefits (freedom to do what you want and when, no issues of how to spend money), though you may find that you become lonely. After all, you're alone in another country; to compound that by exploring alone might be too isolating. If you don't want to travel in a group, another option is to hook up with people along the way. It's easy to make friends with fellow explorers while on the road. Making friends along the way and yet having the freedom of traveling without a group or a combined agenda might be appealing. However, you may have an easier time with communication if you have more heads working on translation of the language and culture than just your own. Traveling as a group can also help with the unease with regard to safety that some students feel.

✳ SAFETY

No matter how well you blend in, tourists are always at a higher risk of being taken advantage of, especially after sunset. Naturally, you must consider safety and available transportation when exploring. Part of the thrill of exploring is the adventure it brings, but ensuring safety is paramount. A safe urban area by day may not be so safe at night. Make sure you don't find yourself in a remote or unpopulated area after sunset, especially if you are alone. If fewer people are on the street, getting assistance in the event of an emergency becomes more difficult. This is especially important to keep in mind if you enjoy discovering places that are less frequented by tourists. Ask local people with whom you are friendly which areas are safe and at what times.

✳ UNDERSTANDING LOCAL SCHEDULING

Try to understand the schedules and how locals interpret them. While some cultures (especially ours) believe that time is money, other cultures have a more laid-back approach. In other words, "things will get done eventually." Public transportation, students tell us, doesn't always leave at the scheduled time. After you miss the first train departing earlier than scheduled, this cultural difference will become very apparent. Political rallies, religious holidays, and neighborhood festivals can also affect your schedule, as can mass transit strikes. Ask locals to forewarn you of such events.

You'll also need to be aware of other logistical challenges, such as:

✈ Adjusting to time changes if you travel outside of your host country's time zone

✈ Making reservations in advance, as some forms of transportation require them and book up quickly

✈ Dealing with crowds if you're using public transportation and if you're visiting the more popular tourist sites during the more popular times of year/day

✈ Understanding procedures for purchasing tickets and making the right decisions on your purchases

✈ Being prepared for weather changes that may affect your plans, especially if you are traveling by boat or plane

✈ Knowing a city's curfew or managing your time to explore if your program also has a curfew

✈ Looking both ways when crossing the street, especially in a country that drives on the opposite side of the street from the United States

Advice for overcoming exploring challenges includes:

✈ Pack a street map.

✈ Learn how to read a rail map.

✈ Write down where you live and where you are going so you can show this to someone if lost.

✈ Keep a travel dictionary with international road signs along with your language dictionary.

✈ Bring snacks in case you are not near any food options.

✈ Allow extra time between transportation transfers.

✈ Dress accordingly if you are visiting religious sites.

✈ Bring the right shoes and adhesive bandages if you will be walking a lot.

✈ Negotiate a fare with a taxi service prior to accepting the ride.

HOW SHOULD YOU PRIORITIZE WHAT TO DO?

As mentioned, one of the biggest challenges with exploring is making the tough choices of what to see and do overseas. With so many options, how will you choose? Again, these decisions will be based on personal preferences and styles as well as what is offered as far as group touring in your program. You also will be limited by time and perhaps by money.

✳ YOUR BUDGET

First, look at your budget to give you a starting point. Research the costs to visit your top points of interest. Consider the price of transportation to and from, lodging, meals, souvenirs, and entrance fees. You might get a special deal on a certain day of the week. Or you might organize a small group if a group rate is available. If you have made friends with locals, perhaps you'll be able to stay with them en route. There are countless ways to save money, but if you really want to save money, you'll have to do the legwork before you leave. Most NSCS students made two lists: "must see" and "would like to see if there's time." This exercise helped keep them in line with their budgets.

✳ SCHEDULING

Decide how you can schedule your "must sees" within your academic schedule. Make sure to ask locals about worthwhile trips that aren't in the typical guidebook. Some NSCS students let the weather be their guide; they would hit the museums in the rain and the parks in the sunshine. If you prefer a slower pace when you explore, allow yourself time to relax at a beach, sip tea by the river, or chat with locals at the newsstand.

✳ PERSONAL PREFERENCES

Determine for yourself how you want to spend time and don't cave in to peer pressure. Whether it's going on "yet another trip to a museum" or "yet another party," following the crowd will be something you regret later. If you don't really want to do something, resist the pressure to do it. We're often told that students who gave themselves time to see sites off the beaten track opened themselves up to more fun and adventure than they would have had on a course laid out by others.

✳ PACKAGED TRIPS

If you'll be on a program that offers planned trips, consider joining some of them. Preplanned group trips often build on years of student experience and can have many advantages, including not waiting in lines to purchase entrance passes, prearranged transportation, and a guide escort. There's also the safety of being in a group. The downsides might be fairly obvious as well. You won't have a "unique" experience. You might be rushed through an area in which you would ideally spend more time. You would have to encounter "tourist traps," sites less authentic than those you'd find on your own. Most NSCS students found a combination of group touring and independent exploring to be the best option for them.

Advice for making the most of your time abroad:

✈ Accept any invitations from trusted locals.

✈ Take plenty of pictures and videos.

✈ Get up early and stay up late.

✈ Don't let the small things get you down.

✈ Get off the beaten track and do as the locals do.

✈ Be outgoing, open, positive, and present.

✈ Focus on your new home and not friends and family members back home.

✈ Try new outdoor local sports.

✈ Go to remote places.

✈ Go for a walk and see where the day takes you.

✈ Pack a sweater and an umbrella.

- Be solid in your morals.

- Find a regular hangout.

- Keep a journal.

- Don't procrastinate.

- Try new things.

- Don't get caught up in the "American scene."

- Don't waste time doing things you can do at home (Internet, TV, etc.).

- Carry your wallet in your front pocket.

- Don't be arrogant about being an American.

- Get to know your host town and surrounding towns intimately; don't try to go too far away every weekend.

- Look for student discounts.

Because you may also have a full course load as a student, have an internship, or be volunteering during the week, make sure to have your schedule reflect enough hours of rest so that your exploring is not a chore but a choice. Exploring can be as simple as sipping cappuccino in a new coffee shop in a neighborhood you don't normally frequent. You might just find these simple explorations to be your most memorable moments overseas, rather than jam-packed days of seeing an array of historical locales. You have chosen to be an exchange student. As such, you will be a student, but one of life as well as the classroom. Your main focus should be to immerse yourself in the new culture, living your life as a native while you are there. This carries with it a lot of personal and sociological exploration. You'll have to make some decisions about what you can't see in the limited time you have abroad, but the good news is, you can always come back.

WHAT SHOULD YOU KNOW ABOUT THE FOOD?

Whether it's with a host family, at a restaurant with new local friends, or in a shared dorm kitchen with fellow exchange students, eating in another culture will be a refreshing experience. All cultures use mealtime as a break from the day to visit with one another. It is not surprising, then, that the kitchen is the center of activity in most, if not all, cultures.

The Numbers

Had a hard time adjusting to the food?

Yes	13%
No	51%

Most NSCS students tell us it's not hard to adjust to the cuisine of their host country. They do, however, have a lot of interesting things to say about the cultural aspects surrounding food. Many of them have as much to do with the routine as the food itself.

✳ DURATION OF MEALS

Meals tend to be much longer than in the United States. Families abroad eat together and sit for hours on end. As a natural consequence, snacking is not very common. Though it took some time, NSCS students grew to enjoy the idea of relaxing for longer periods (two to four hours) over foods prepared well in advance.

In many cultures, taking an afternoon break is a ritual taken with colleagues, friends, or family; it can be a half-day event.

✳ TIMING OF MEALS

Meals tend to be held late in the day. Though times vary, lunch occurs closer to 2:00 PM or 3:00 PM, and dinner starts closer to 9:00 PM or 10:00 PM. Breakfast may be smaller than you are used to at home, with lunch being the largest meal and dinner a light snack. Students in England often attended tea time around 4:00 PM in addition to their regular meals.

"Time seems to be perceived a bit differently in Vienna, as it is in many parts of Europe. The first settlement here came into existence over two thousand years ago, so what's a year, a decade, even a century in the grand scheme of things? In Vienna cafés, lingering over one's drink isn't just accepted—it's expected and almost mandated by etiquette. Every cup of tea or coffee is accompanied by a small (we're talking six ounces) glass of water. If and when you drink this water, you will be brought another one, gratis.

In this manner, you can spend all day in the café and remain perfectly hydrated, all for the price of one cup of coffee. Such a laid-back atmosphere shows a lack of obsessive concern for capitalist efficiency. It is a way of life more conducive to producing intellectuals than über-businessmen or inventors."

Dmitriy Zakharov
Mobile, AL
Georgetown University

✳ MEAL PREPARATION AND INGREDIENTS

Food preparation abroad might come as a surprise. Countries such as France, which hold the culinary arts in high esteem, take a great deal of pride in serving fancy meals for longer periods of time. In Poland, an NSCS student found herself eating more fried food than she was used to at home. Drinking beer or wine at lunch was also common in instances where the drink was intended to bring out the flavors of the food. Overall, students found that they were eating more carbohydrates, more meats, and just plain "healthier" while they were overseas, with fewer processed food options. Spices also affected students' experiences: Those in England complained that the food tasted bland, while those in Thailand enjoyed some of the spicier dishes. NSCS students also report trying things that are unfamiliar, such as octopus or fish with the head still on.

✳ TABLE MANNERS AND ETIQUETTE

Table manners vary from country to country, as does utensil use. For example, some cultures do not value a cleaned plate, while others insist upon it. Though you are not mandated to adopt the local mannerisms, you might find it fun to try. The best way to blend in is first to observe others. You might even find that slurping and burping are encouraged! Some examples are:

✈ Holding a knife in the right hand and a fork upside down in the left at all times (Germany)

✈ Eating sausage informally with no plate but with a beer in hand (Australia)

✈ Eating communally with your hands (Thailand)

✈ Tearing, not cutting, bread (France)

✈ Looking each other in the eye while toasting (Germany)

✈ Keeping one hand on the table (Spain)

✳ CUSTOMER SERVICE AND TIPPING

Customer service in restaurants varies significantly by country, and so does tipping. In many countries, tipping is simply a small gesture of thanks, not the established practice to which Americans are accustomed. As such, waiters may be less focused on "American-style" customer service. Catching a waiter's eye to ask for more water or the bill might be a challenge. The server might, instead, be looking for your clues, such as utensils placed in the four and eight o'clock positions on your plate, before bringing your check. And in countries where tips are nominal, you might be charged for the bread that is presented on every table or for just sitting at the table. And finally, showing appreciation to the chef may not cross all cultures, but if you are in certain countries, it is imperative you do so.

✳ SPECIAL DIETS

Vegetarian and vegan students have had some issues maintaining their diet overseas, especially in countries where people consume a lot of meat. If you have any food allergies or special needs, it is important to clarify them up front. Rejecting food served to you can be considered rude in many cultures, and you wouldn't want to cause an awkward misunderstanding.

Other differences with regard to eating overseas include:

✈ The temperature of drinks (and the infrequent use of ice)

✈ Meats and fish served raw

✈ Ketchup used on many food items

✈ Meat prepared differently and with different sanitation guidelines

✈ The practice of napping after a midday meal

✈ Eating "family style"

✈ Fighting over who pays the bill and the social etiquette around this custom

✈ Refrigeration not used for some items, such as milk, eggs, or meat

✈ Grocery shopping done daily

✈ Sparkling water instead of flat

✈ The protocol for how much to eat and when to stop eating what is served to you

"For October break from the University of Delhi, in India, I had 17 incredible days of adventuring out on my own. I started by going to Jaisalmere, an amazingly beautiful city in the desert made entirely from a yellow sandstone that gives it an almost golden glow. The real reason I went to Jaisalmere was to go on a camel safari—camels are awesome! I rode through the desert for three days and would have gone on for longer if I hadn't been getting so very sunburned. The desert was fascinating, scenic, and so fresh and clean after life in Delhi. The evenings were the best part: making *chapatti* (flat wheat bread), chai, rice, and subzee (vegetables) over the fire; singing and telling stories; and falling asleep under a sky full of so many stars you could see falling stars and the Milky Way.

I left the camels in Jodhpur, a much bigger and picturesque city filled with squarish buildings painted blue. Jodhpur Fort is really interesting, especially the defenses, which include tight corners designed to prevent elephant charges and many different cannons on the ramparts.

From there, it was the night train on to Mumbai. Mumbai is great. You get there and it seems like Europe—there are huge gothic buildings everywhere. I spent the day wandering and admiring buildings and then headed to Chowpatty beach, the center of Mumbai nightlife. Everyone is out on the beach: families, couples, the elderly, the poor washing their clothes, and the upper class watching the sunset. Then there are the vendors—*wallas*—selling all kinds of things. The next day, I headed out and ran into a man asking if I would like to be in a Bollywood movie, so I spent the whole day as an extra dancing in an old abandoned night club. Then I was off to Elephanta Island, which has these amazingly carved rock caves full of Hindu gods, the most amazing being a bust of five-headed Shiva eight meters high. On my way back from the island, I ran into another Bollywood agent who wanted me to go right then to a shoot. After finishing that scene, the three of us extras went out to this really big traditional dance festival with thousands of people, and we danced the night away!

I finally headed back home to Delhi on a 24-hour train ride, where I had time to contemplate all I had seen on my adventure; it was certainly an experience I'll never forget."

Alison Cleary
San Fransisco, CA
University of California, San Diego

HOW CAN YOU GET THE MOST OUT OF YOUR FREE TIME?

According to our sources at NSCS, about half of students take advantage of programs that offer weekend excursions. They overwhelmingly recommend these experiences. Some programs require that you take the trips and charge you up front for the costs involved, while most programs have optional weekend opportunities. Some trips are organized by the professors of the program, other trips are set up by outside organizations, but most are run by the college or university sponsoring the program.

These types of programs are often quite popular at the beginning, when students are new to the country, but less popular over time. As students feel more comfortable planning their own excursions, they branch out more on their own. Students highly recommend these programs, however. The activities are "amazing opportunities" that are well thought out and fun to do as a group. Going as a group, the rates might be better negotiated, the logistics arranged so you don't have to worry about them, and getting into some events may be easier. Students also felt that these group excursions were a great way to get to know other students more intimately and helped when they were feeling homesick. However, some students found that their weekend programs were disorganized and limiting. Some also complained of feeling as though they were on an elementary school field trip.

Some students chose not to participate because they preferred to sleep in, could not afford to, were too late in signing up and the seats were limited, or were sick. However, if you have the opportunity, students would recommend you sign up for as many trips as you find interesting. Very few students did not find them rewarding and fun!

Some examples of weekend getaways:

+ Attending a bullfight during the San Fermin Festival in Pamplona, Spain

+ Learning the tango in Uruguay

+ Visiting the Vatican in Vatican City, Italy

+ Being serenaded by a gondolier on the Grand Canal in Venice, Italy

+ Watching a guitar concert in the Opera House in Hanoi, Vietnam

+ Performing on the stage with Czechoslovakian conductors

+ Attending a traditional dinner in Panama

+ Going shopping in the outdoor market in Otavalo, Ecuador

+ Touring the European Commission, the European Parliament, and the Council of the European Union in Brussels, Belgium

+ Hiking in the Andes of Spain

Exploring Your New Surroundings   129

NSCS TAKE-ABROADS

✈ Getting around comes with some obstacles, but for the most part, it is fairly easy if you do your research.

✈ When you go about deciding what to do, you'll want to factor in time, money, and your own personal interests.

✈ There is no right way to explore, but knowing your personal preferences will help you decide if you want to go out on your own, take a group tour, or travel with friends who have a similar agenda.

✈ Eating overseas is just one of the cultural experiences you'll encounter, but it may be the best way to see how families and friends abroad interact.

✈ Make the most of every weekend and the free time you are given. This time is just as, if not more, important to your experiential learning than the time you spend in the classroom.

CHAPTER

7

Gaining Experience

"Volunteering at a community center in Buenos Aires was such an eye-opening experience for me, because it allowed me to see the stark differences between the urban parts of Buenos Aires and the poorer streets filled with homeless women and children just a few blocks away. At the community center, my group's task was to create a library for the children who wanted help with their English. But while working, some of us often felt helpless because we wanted to do so much more but were limited by the language barrier. Working at the community center definitely reinforced the importance of understanding Spanish."

Mindy L.
Athens, Georgia
The University of Georgia

Whether through a formal internship program, living with a host family, volunteering, or exploring on the weekends, immersion is key if you are to make the most of your time abroad. The level at which you are immersed in your host culture is a choice. As many students who have studied overseas will tell you, you can make the experience as rich as you want it to be: You are overseas both to learn and to be an ambassador of your own country, and you can't very well do either if you're in front of your computer or listening to music on your headphones. Getting out into the community is the best way to make the most of your short time abroad.

HOW CAN YOU GET IMMERSED IN THE CULTURE?

A deeper level of immersion in any culture is the difference between being a tourist and being a community member. (In fact, deep immersion may make your transition back home harder. Many students experience reverse culture shock when returning home, though all of them say the experience was well worth it.) Here's some advice for successful immersion into a new culture.

✳ GET OUT OF YOUR COMFORT ZONE

Resist the strong temptation to stay within your comfort zone. This means not spending all your time with other Americans and not going to every party that's thrown. Get off the beaten path, and you will be rewarded with new foods, friends, and vocabulary. Successfully immersed students report that life was totally different overseas, with much less Internet, phone, or TV. By not doing as much of these things, their time was freed up to step out into their new world.

132   ✪   Adventures Abroad

"Another American girl, Tabitha, asked me to go with her to Cape Town. She had some friends there who were coming to pick her up, and she wanted somebody to come along for moral support, so I agreed, and we were off. However, what I thought would be a routine ride turned out to be anything but. The entire ride was an educational experience to say the least. We took a combi (Volkswagen bus) with four completely strange guys who were Xhosa speakers, and soon after we departed, the language lessons began in full force. They also taught me a lot about the race dynamics of Stellenbosch, Kayamandi, Cape Town, and Kayalitsha, through an odd assortment of jokes, stories, and personal experiences.

I had noticed as much uncertainty on Tabitha's face as on my own as we boarded the combi, but as we arrived in Cape Town, we felt all the more enlightened by these guys and their music and jokes. They were an unexpected fount of information regarding the dynamics of this place of extreme social complexity."

Rebekah Hartnett
Manhattan, KS
University of Kansas

✳ MAKE A FRIEND

If you can make even just one local friend, your social experience will significantly open up. Any friend you make will have other friends to whom he or she will introduce you. You may soon find yourself being asked to join a large group of locals. All of these people can help you with your immersion. Making friends in any country takes time—in a short-term program, it's even harder—but it can be done. Also, if it helps your confidence, reach out together with a fellow student. The two of you can lean on each other until you connect more individually with the locals.

✳ DON'T CLING TO HOME

Let go of daily interactions with home. You will need to find other sources of comfort while you are overseas if you truly want to become immersed. This does not mean that you will love or appreciate your family and friends at home less; it simply means that you will expand your network to include your host country friends. By cutting ties with home for the short time you are overseas, you will free up more time to make native friends, giving yourself the mental energy to redirect your focus and priorities. You'll also keep your language learning going without interruption.

✳ TALK TO STRANGERS

Don't be afraid to communicate with strangers. Your first reaction might be to pull back from a situation that is so new. With study abroad, however, interaction with locals is your key to growth and discovery. Remember, too, that friends can come in all shapes and sizes. Talk with people who are different from you in age, socioeconomic status, ethnicity, etc. Push yourself out of your comfort zone.

134 ✿ Adventures Abroad

✳ LAUGH AT YOURSELF

Learn to have a thick skin and laugh at yourself. You will make mistakes and you will ask obvious questions, but you will grow and learn. You'll also survive embarrassment if you can laugh it off and realize it's all part of being an exchange student.

✳ BE SPONTANEOUS

Listing all you would like to accomplish so that you can plan your time is a great idea, but leave yourself time for unplanned events. New experiences are sure to present themselves to you. NSCS students recommend that if you are a planner, you should plan some time to get lost!

✳ TRY SOMETHING NEW

Get involved in things you might not have been interested in at home. Just like food, you might like it if you try it. Fear can also inhibit your learning the language and asking questions to understand something better. Remember, too, that saying no to an invitation is considered highly rude in some cultures. As the saying goes, "When in Rome, do as the Romans do." If your host country is known for its operas, you'll want to find out why; if your host country has renowned cheeses, you'll want to taste them to understand the appeal.

"Mahatma Gandhi, a truly tolerant individual, clearly explained religious diversity when he stated, 'If we are to respect others' religions as we would have them respect our own, a friendly study of the world's religions is a sacred duty.' Replacing the word *religion* in this quotation with *race, culture,* or *social class* would convey the same message.

I have taken the advice of Gandhi and embarked on a 'friendly study.' Over a period of four months, I have studied on different ends of the Earth, taking part in numerous medical education programs. What I learned in these experiences reached far beyond any medical textbook. I studied Spanish in Spain, impoverished societies in Nicaragua, and various herbal remedies in Costa Rica. Each of these cultural studies clearly contributed to my understanding of diversity, but what really allowed me to relate to the issue that Gandhi and others have portrayed was my Buddhist immersion experience in the rural town of Singburi, Thailand.

This month-long experience was not a vacation in Thailand; it was a service. I headed there alone to join a small group of volunteers and Global Service Corps, and we then went off to spend a night in Buddhist Wat Songpithong. Our translator there guided us each step of the way and related to us what the head monk, the abbot, was saying. We changed into the appropriate white attire in a closet-sized bathroom with only a bucket for all washing and excreting purposes, and we barely ate any dinner, as the monks at Wat Songpithong only eat one early meal a day in an effort to maintain vitality for the remainder of it. Around seven o'clock in the evening, we joined the monks in the temple to chant before retiring to sleep on a barren floor alongside our fellow insect counterparts.

At 4:00 AM, we woke to chant again. Both chanting sessions were accompanied by circumstances that would have been difficult to fathom for any person preoccupied by modern American culture. For over an hour, we kneeled on hard cement floors and straw mats in an effort to keep our feet pointed away from the Buddha statue that stood before us. All the while, the insects that shared the floor space with us crawled over our feet and legs, some even making it up to our white blouses before we noticed the stinging pinches they gave. In order to enjoy, or at least respect, the moment, we truly had to heed the words of the Buddhists: Regardless of our individual beliefs, we must detach ourselves from the circumstances. I achieved a higher state of being at the very moment I came to realize that I was in a room filled with people, volunteers, and monks of all backgrounds and appearances, sharing that same moment. The diversity grazed the room like paint on the canvas of a beautiful work of art; without the variety of colors, shapes, and gradations, it would not have been so influential."

Robin Ortiz
Edison, NJ
Northeastern University

Other suggestions for getting immersed:

✈ Choose to live with a host family if given the option.

✈ Join a club that you would, or would not, consider joining if you were at home.

✈ Go to sporting events and concerts.

✈ Take a dance class.

✈ Take a train ride out of the city to a town you have never heard of.

✈ Take a cooking class.

✈ Go to the street festivals.

✈ Go to a movie in the foreign language you are learning.

✈ Become a "regular" and get to know a shop owner.

✈ Find a language tutor.

✈ Take a class that isn't offered at home.

✈ Join a gym or yoga class.

NSCS students have also shared their regrets. They wish they had done:

- ✈ Walked around the city more

- ✈ Volunteered

- ✈ Visited more places in the country

- ✈ Focused more on the present than the future

- ✈ Gotten to know their host families better

- ✈ Picked a program that was longer in duration

- ✈ Taken one fewer class and used the time to explore

- ✈ Gone on the program alone and not with friends from home

- ✈ Spent less time in their room

Give yourself daily or weekly goals so that you get involved in a measured way. Even if you're tired, try to push yourself to keep going, while staying healthy. By the same token, allow yourself only a certain amount of time to be in your room. You'll always wish you had done more.

138 ✿ Adventures Abroad

SHOULD YOU TAKE AN INTERNSHIP?

A growing number of students participate in internship programs while they live overseas, and many programs are designed this way. Some internships are optional, and some are mandatory. If you don't receive assistance from your university/college program office in selecting an internship location, you can do your own online research and self-promotion (though if you want to find the internship yourself, you'll likely have to spend time making connections in your host country well in advance of your program).

NSCS students have taken internships in a variety of industries. Examples include:

- ✈ Assisting in the delivery of babies in a hospital in the Philippines

- ✈ Being a teacher's aid in a school in France

- ✈ Coaching a basketball team in the Dominican Republic

- ✈ Working in public relations for an orphanage in Brazil

- ✈ Doing international marketing in Spain

- ✈ Researching energy, the environment, and biotechnology with local leaders in Malta

- ✈ Aiding lawyers in a legal office in England

Gaining Experience   ✿   139

Internship structures vary depending on your program. Some are a combination of classes and the internship, with weeks assigned for each, and others assign certain hours of each day for classes and the internship. The time commitment needed for internships also varies, from a few hours a week to full-time (40 hours), depending on the program's structure. If you choose to find an internship on your own without the help of your program, make sure you get it approved by your institution before leaving so that you'll be sure you earn the credits you need.

Students who participate in internship programs find the experience to be very rewarding. The intangible benefits of internships are numerous. You can do the following:

✈ Gain hands-on experience in interviewing

✈ Get prepared for future job searches after school

✈ Add international work to your resume (which will help you stand out in years to come)

✈ Form friendships with new colleagues

✈ Learn about the culture from an inside perspective

✈ Gain real-world employment experience

✈ Have easier access to return to your host country later through the connections you make

✈ Understand the ethics in the workplace of your host country

✈ Commute like a local during rush hour

✈ Participate in something for which you have a passion

"Let's just say that, at least in Prague, internships are taken way more seriously than in the United States. I observed firsthand the demand for native English speakers is quite high for any organization that publishes for an international audience."

Dmitriy Zakharov
Mobile, AL
Georgetown University

One of the more tangible benefits of an internship program is being paid a stipend or at least travel benefits. Though many internships are unpaid, a few do provide small stipends or travel money to get to and from the office. This money certainly could help boost your budget for weekend excursions. Another benefit is the occasional work trip that interns are asked to take, allowing you to see more of your host country firsthand. If your internship proves to be a positive experience for both you and the employer, you may be able to return there for a job after you've completed your studies.

With any internship, here or abroad, be prepared to perform some menial tasks. An internship isn't the place you're going to tackle major assignments, but it is an experience you'll find highly rewarding even so. Project work is bound to be more multidimensional, including different perspectives from your home and host cultures. Also, it will help you solidify your language skills and give you more of a direction for your future major or career path. NSCS students will tell you that interning overseas "takes your experience to the next level," or that it is "beyond words," "immeasurable," and "priceless."

Gaining Experience   143

SHOULD YOU VOLUNTEER?

Many students have neither the opportunity nor the time to volunteer when they're abroad. Those who were lucky enough to volunteer, however, say it's a worthwhile activity. You'll feel less like a tourist and more like a true local.

Volunteering allows you to feel proud of your contribution with no expectations of getting something back. Imagine volunteering at home: the rewards are many. Now imagine volunteering in another country: the rewards are many and vastly more interesting.

Volunteering overseas is often done in small groups so that goals are group-oriented. Community development is usually the focus, specifically in areas of public assistance. Once you have volunteered for a period of time, you may find that the experience helps to motivate you toward a goal. Because the time you will be abroad is limited, it might be difficult to get too involved in any long-term volunteer project; but even for a short time, any volunteering is time well spent.

"I wanted to find a charity in Cape Town that the Organization of African Students at George Washington University could support by sending money, books, clothing, or other handouts. Once I actually got to South Africa, however, and saw the orphanages and the poverty in the townships, I realized that as much as a handout is a good thing, it is not the only thing that should be done to help those in need. I began to see that those handouts only help for the moment, and in turn make the people that much more dependent on privileged foreigners.

I learned that the alternative was empowerment and education. I was able to see this firsthand when I got involved with the University of Cape Town's Township Debate League (TDL), the purpose of which was to teach high school students debating skills. My friends and I liked volunteering at TDL, because instead of giving out money or handouts, we were able to help empower young people and share knowledge with the future generations of South Africa.

After one semester, so many of the students were more confident, had a better command of English, and understood the basics of a simple argument. These are skills that are going to be very useful to them in the future. The program has been in place for three years, and already some of the initial students from the first year will be attending the University of Cape Town and will go back to their high schools to continue to build on what TDL has already established. Educating people in the skills they need to succeed is what must happen on a larger scale to promote development and growth throughout Africa. I am glad that I was able to be a small part of that for the short time that I spent studying abroad."

Esther Agbaje
Portsmouth, Virginia
The George Washington University

Gaining Experience ✪ 145

Volunteer opportunities could include:

➤ Assisting a nonprofit worker with research of nocturnal frogs in Puerto Rico

➤ Working with middle school students in Chile

➤ Raising awareness of less fortunate children in Norway

➤ Serving dinner at a retirement home in Spain

➤ Playing games with elementary school children in Japan

➤ Traveling in a mobile clinic as a premed student in South Africa

➤ Teaching Sunday school classes in Germany

➤ Planting thousands of trees in watershed areas in New Zealand

Though you are giving of yourself when you volunteer, you are also gaining in many ways. Just as with an internship, you'll gain real-world experience, more advanced language learning, friendships with locals, and a nice overseas experience to add to your resume. In some cases, you might be able to obtain free housing if you wanted to stay on longer after the program. Some NSCS students regret not having opened themselves to volunteer opportunities while they were overseas.

NSCS TAKE-ABROADS

✈ Many programs offer internships overseas; the amount of work time varies from program to program.

✈ Students who volunteered or interned overseas greatly enriched their overall experiences.

✈ Volunteering or interning will assist in your immersion in your host culture.

✈ Making native friends, learning the language, trying the foods, and learning the politics and pop culture are just a few ways in which you can immerse yourself in your host country's culture.

✈ Immersion is a big part of the learning you will do as an exchange student; it is up to you how much or little you get involved in your host culture.

CHAPTER 8

Safety

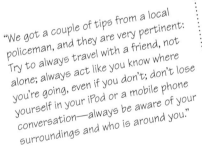

"We got a couple of tips from a local policeman, and they are very pertinent: Try to always travel with a friend, not alone; always act like you know where you're going, even if you don't; don't lose yourself in your iPod or a mobile phone conversation—always be aware of your surroundings and who is around you."

Whitney E.
Churubusco, Indiana
Indiana University—Bloomington

Safety is an issue wherever you are living. It may also be your parents' primary concern for your time abroad. The adventure of living and exploring an unknown culture, land, and language is challenge enough; add any anxiety about safety, and you're headed for serious stress. It is possible, however, to manage the concerns so that both you and your family are comfortable.

DEALING WITH THE ISSUE OF CRIME

When asked whether they felt unsafe overseas, more than half of all NSCS students answered with a resounding *no*: They never felt unsafe while abroad. Japan and Australia, in particular, were cited for safety; crime rates there are much lower than in the United States. What gave students a sense of security? The fact that their schools overseas had their best interests at heart, faith in a higher power, confidence in their own abilities, and the fact that the U.S. State Department knew their whereabouts.

The Numbers

Felt unsafe abroad?

Sometimes	32%
No	56%
Yes	12%

---

150 ❂ **Adventures Abroad**

"Be aware of your surroundings and stay in groups, especially if you go out at night; be particularly cautious at nightclubs. Don't make it obvious that you are a foreigner. Be careful with what you say and how you secure your belongings. Always establish the price with a taxi driver before you get into their vehicle, and never get into an unofficial taxi."

Tracy C.
Fairfield, VA
James Madison University

5¢

Safety   151

For those students who tell us they felt unsafe, the majority cited everything from minor crimes to the threat of terrorism in mass transit. A few students did in fact have their pockets picked, and a few report being harassed. But these were the extreme minority. As a tourist, your culture could betray you and make it impossible to blend in. Your distinctiveness will make you stand out, something that comes with all the positives and negatives associated with "being different." Because foreigners can be a target in any country, it follows that train stations and tourist spots are areas of risk.

Some students felt that a disconnect between languages, both verbal and nonverbal, was a factor in their feeling unsafe. When they didn't understand the meaning behind others' actions, their anxieties rose. In one's native culture, it may be easier to detect something that doesn't feel "right" than it is overseas.

"Upon arrival in Kiev, I made my way from the train station to the adjacent metro stop, where I was promptly stopped by a policeman who asked to see my papers. Perhaps I really looked like I was not a local, or perhaps a recently arrived young man with bags and a short haircut has 'I'm running from something' written all over him. Regardless, I was sure to be polite and accommodating, and after having been satisfied that I was not, in fact, skipping out on Ukrainian military service or anything of the like, he wished me luck, and I made my way into the metro."

Dmitriy Zakharov
Mobile, AL
Georgetown University

TIPS FOR A SAFE ADVENTURE ABROAD

First and foremost, use your instincts the way you would use them at home. Predators know that as a foreigner, you have a handicap with communication. If you are a woman, don't walk alone. If you are going to take an overnight train somewhere, don't do it alone. In short, don't let your guard down. Here are some more tips.

✳ PLAN TO GET HOME

Don't travel in unknown areas at night. If you know you're going to be out of town for the day, or in some remote part of town, make plans to get home in advance. You don't want to get stuck in an unfamiliar location with no way to get home. Bigger cities (and more impoverished areas) tend to be more dangerous than smaller towns—though that doesn't mean small towns don't see some crime.

✳ LOCAL LAW ENFORCEMENT

Be aware that police overseas might use tactics that are less common at home. Tear gas might be used on large public gatherings, or police may appear heavily armed. Some female students tell us they didn't always feel safe going to the police over concerns of corruption, though most students felt that large-scale safety was handled in a well-controlled, systematic, and orderly fashion.

✳ ANTI-AMERICAN SENTIMENT

You may experience anti-American sentiment directed at either the U.S. government or U.S. policies in general. Some students found that agreeing with those criticisms in one-to-one conversations helped to soften the antagonism in the air. (A few students have even gone so far as to pretend to be Canadian.) While political demonstrations are interesting to watch, make sure you observe from afar. If the situation were to become volatile, you want to make sure you're a safe distance away. Oftentimes, U.S. citizens serve as scapegoats for others, and it's best not to engage in contentious political conversations. In short, change the subject.

✳ CLOSENESS AND TOUCHING

The proximity factor also is a consideration when speaking about safety. If someone is standing too close for your comfort, anxieties rise. Students tell us they felt unsafe when these situations went to the next level—if someone touched their hair or face. This seemed rather common in airports, where vendors who were selling rooms for rent, souvenirs, or taxis would come very close to get students' attention.

✳ UNDERSTAND THE LOCAL MONEY

Be careful that you aren't taken advantage of with small currency. Some students told us that vendors occasionally did not return the correct change or would charge an unnecessarily higher price. Get familiar with the way the foreign currency works before you go out shopping. Plus, be discreet with your cash. Don't flash large sums of money for people to see.

✳ STAY UP-TO-DATE ON LOCAL CONDITIONS

The U.S. government monitors on a daily basis the political conditions in every country of the world. Go to travel.state.gov to check on the conditions of the country you intend to visit. This is the U.S. State Department's website, which is updated frequently. You can also call 888-407-4747, the State Department's new toll-free number with up-to-the-minute travel warnings for any country. You should read also the consular information sheet (available at travel.state. gov) for the country you plan to visit. It will include such information as the location of the U.S. Embassy or Consulate in the host country, health conditions, minor political disturbances, unusual currency and entry regulations, crime and security information, and drug penalties.

✳ TAKING A CAB

Negotiate taxi prices before getting into the car. Ask the driver before you leave about the approximate cost of travel to avoid being driven in circles so as to hike up the fare. Obviously, you want to avoid a dispute with your driver, and above all, you don't want a situation that escalates to violence. This can be avoided if you agree on price beforehand. And be wary altogether of drivers who are too aggressive in soliciting business.

156 ❂ Adventures Abroad

✳ **YOUR IMPORTANT DOCUMENTS**

Keep in mind that your passport can be as enticing as money. Keep the original in your room and carry a photocopy on you, preferably in a hidden pouch or pocket. Make a list of your travelers check and credit card numbers, as well, and keep those at home.

Advice for keeping safe:

✈ Don't draw too much attention to yourself.

✈ Have a plan in place in case you lose an important document (such as your passport or credit card) or it is stolen.

✈ If a safe is provided, store your money and valuables in it.

✈ Always have a plan to meet in case someone gets lost.

✈ Carry money in several places on your physical person (use a money belt).

✈ Trust your instincts.

✈ Never leave a drink unattended.

✈ Don't take shortcuts.

✈ Don't talk about "how rich Americans are."

✈ Don't wear flashy jewelry.

- Program the police into your cell phone in case of emergencies.

- Ignore flirtatious advances if you don't want to interact with the person.

- Know the location of the nearest hospital.

- Don't take rides from strangers.

- Be extra cautious at ATM machines.

- Always let someone know where you're going and how to reach your loved ones in case of emergency.

- Stand up for yourself, or flee, as the circumstance requires.

- Always know how to get home from a location, especially at night.

- Watch yourself around train stations at night.

- Try to blend in with the way you dress.

- If you are waiting for mass transportation in an area that feels unsafe, take a taxi instead.

- Read about the safe and unsafe areas in a guidebook before exploring.

✈ Talk with your school officials about your fears.

✈ Never sleep alone on a train.

✈ Bring your travel insurance card.

✈ Know the location of the nearest embassy or consulate.

✈ Always have a map on you.

✈ If you're being followed, walk steadfastly to a police station.

✈ Don't be confrontational.

✈ Know your comfort limits (a day trip alone, for example).

✈ Don't have your earphones on or talk on your cell phone without paying attention to your surroundings.

✈ Avoid participating in rallies or marches. Watch from a distance.

✈ Carry a whistle on your key chain.

✈ Obey the laws of the country.

Bad neighborhoods exist everywhere. If something does happen, don't blame yourself. Learn what you can from the experience so that you are safer next time. Knowing where and when you should be in a certain part of town is one of the keys to staying safe. You will want to take all necessary precautions and to be realistic, but then not allow fear to take over your experience.

NSCS TAKE-ABROADS

✈ Generally speaking, students did not feel unsafe overseas.

✈ To stay safe anywhere, you need to be vigilant about your surroundings.

✈ Knowing the language and culture will help you to interpret events around you correctly and determine whether a situation is unsafe or just different.

✈ Be proactive about safety: Know how you'll get home after dark, program emergency numbers into your cell phone, and make copies of important documents.

✈ Ask the locals about which areas to avoid. Try to blend in so you don't become a target for criminals, especially pickpockets.

CHAPTER

9

Being a U.S. Ambassador

"While studying abroad at Delhi University, a dorm mate asked me, 'What is Halloween? Is it like on One Tree Hill?' Rather than attempting to explain all that was great about Halloween, a few other American students and I decided to show our dorm mates firsthand.

So October 28 (the 31st is a major religious holiday in India) was our dorm's Spooktacular Halloween Party. In the preceding days, we had planned and prepared to roll all the American party traditions into one big Halloween. We spent the whole day making paper jack-o-lanterns and tissue ghosts, and cooking 'graveyard' pudding and caramel corn for the hundred girls in the residence.

At first, it seemed a little awkward, but as more people started arriving and admiring each other's costumes, it really became a proper Halloween. What was great was that since you can't buy any costumes or even any face paint in Delhi, people were really creative with their costumes. As part of a scary costume, one girl burned newspaper and covered half her face with the black from that, then covered the other half of her face with toothpaste. We had a jack-o-lantern piñata, which was good fun—none of the other girls had ever hit a piñata—and even our warden had a try! It ended being a great time, and now our dorm mates will never again have to wonder what Halloween is really like."

NSCS Memeber
Baton Rouge, LA
Louisianna State University

Depending on when you travel overseas, the political climate might dictate the way in which you are treated as an American. The popularity of the U.S. culture ebbs and flows around the world, and you need to be prepared for different reactions. NSCS students tell us that people assign anti-American sentiment in many ways: toward U.S. political actions, current administration personalities, the president himself, or the West in general. While some populations might love American products, they might also hold the United States responsible for many of the world's problems. Both sentiments—love and hate—could together make the relationships you have overseas complex and the conversations more spirited.

DEALING WITH ANTI-AMERICANISM

While you are overseas, you will inevitably have to serve as a de facto ambassador for the United States. This means helping to explain U.S. policies and culture and clarifying the difference between "official" America and Americans as people. If your experience is similar to that of NSCS students, you'll find anti-Americanism displayed on a personal level—mostly in jokes, sarcasm, or words that don't escalate into anything more than emotionally charged ideas. On a public level, you may witness protests, see graffiti, or watch strikes against the United States and its policies. Most events are harmless and nonviolent; however, spirited conversations could turn tense. Some students were spit at or yelled at for no other reason but their national identity. Others were denied service by cabdrivers or waitstaff. However, these experiences are rare. Above all, realize that most people around the world want simply to express their opinions about the state of international affairs. Try to take it in stride without taking it too personally.

American domestic and foreign policies are something with which most host country nationals are familiar, and they do not hesitate to voice their opinions. Classmates, or even complete strangers, may deride all Americans (or even you personally!), either to irritate you or out of prejudice or ignorance. Many students found themselves at a loss for words or uncomfortable in these discussions. They found themselves unprepared and without the knowledge to defend their viewpoints. If you are preparing to study abroad, make sure you educate yourself beforehand about the big-ticket issues going on in our country (if you don't already know).

You'll want to be prepared to hear some resentment based on the following:

✈ The leadership of the United States

✈ The U.S. role of "world police"

✈ Western lifestyles and attitudes

✈ American fast food chains spreading and polluting the good health of a nation

You might also experience stereotyping. After all, many of the people in your host country will have seen Americans only on TV or film, and they have no firsthand knowledge of what life in the United States is really like. Some people believe all Americans are fat, loud, rude, and lazy. Others might believe them to be unintelligent, materialistic, and arrogant—or friendly, smiley, and hardworking. It is your job to explain to your host country friends that some—if not all—of these stereotypes are false. Some NSCS students tell us that to counter the stereotype that Americans are loud, for example, they made sure to be extra quiet and demure.

The Numbers

Witnessed other American students
representing the United States in a bad way?

Yes	34%
No	27%

Had the opportunity to talk to
foreigners about American culture?

Yes	51%
No	11%

HOW SHOULD YOU COUNTER ANTI-AMERICAN SENTIMENTS?

So what's the best way to handle people who display resentment or criticism toward the United States? NSCS students recommend the following:

✈ Take the time to sit down and have a real conversation with any critics you meet (assuming the environment is safe). People who might purport to dislike America or Americans on the whole have trouble applying these prejudices face-to-face, on an individual basis.

✈ Brush up on your knowledge of your host country's government and cultural history before you go. If you have an idea of the norms and beliefs that pervade it, you'll be able to put the discussions in context. Political conversations can escalate quickly into heated debates, and it is up to you as the unofficial ambassador of your nation to remain calm and listen.

✈ Answer questions to the best of your ability and explain that you are only one citizen. Naturally, your own personal beliefs may or may not be in line with the government's actions. Letting the person venting frustration know that you agree with their opinion also helps to allay emotions.

- Don't take things personally. Realize that peoples' complaints are often the result of national priorities or biased information. There's no personal anger toward you—a student—and most people make it clear that they're criticizing the administration in general.

- Keep informed of the news back home. It's easy to get caught up in a reality bubble while you're overseas, but do try to stay abreast of significant events at home. Any news website will provide the information you need. Try to read local news in your host country (most countries have English-language newspapers) as well as American websites based at home. You'll find it refreshing to see the difference in how they each approach the news. News reported overseas tends to be far more global/international than news in the United States.

- Be twice as polite as you would be normally. People will be more likely to process what you are saying if you are calm and courteous. Learn the proper customs so as not to embarrass yourself or offend anyone.

Try to be proud of who you are and where you come from. Turn the other cheek if you are made to feel intimidated. While anti-American sentiment exists, see it as part of your growth toward becoming an informal ambassador for your country.

"There is a lot of anti-American sentiment abroad, even in places that you think would be more accepting of our culture. It can be extremely frustrating to have to try to explain or defend our culture, especially if you don't speak the language well enough!

It isn't something you can always control, either. For example, there was a copy of Michelangelo's La Pieta being shown in Venice, but this particular copy featured an American flag beneath the religious figures of Mary and Jesus. While viewing the statue in a place with tourists from all nations, we bore witness to many negative comments toward Americans and about our nation. We wanted so badly to say something in defense of America, even if it was just to say that we didn't necessarily agree with the artist's choice to associate one particular nation with one of the most famous religious figures in the world. But we decided it was better to let it alone and not cause any problems. You can't change everyone's way of thinking, but you can set an example and try to change the negative stereotypes other people have of Americans."

Emily Marzullo
Highland, California
University of California—Riverside

Many students, of course, speak with their host country friends about the American culture—and about the differences between the two cultures—on topics ranging from politics to pop culture. NSCS students were asked about the following issues.

✳ CURRENT WORLD POLITICS

✈ Their own views on politics, the U.S. president, and current U.S. actions around the world

✈ Their own views on Hitler and World War II (Germany)

✈ Why Americans are so "arrogant" in their foreign relations

✈ The actions and motivations of the U.S. president

✈ Why the United States seems so ambivalent about joining in the fight to protect the environment

170　◎　Adventures Abroad

※ MOVIES AND TELEVISION

➤ How real life in the United States compares to that seen on television

➤ What U.S. culture is other than materialism, Hollywood, and fast food

Also, since movies and televisions are the primary channels by which many people form opinions of American culture, students often found themselves compared to celebrities and actors.

※ DAILY LIFE

➤ Why Americans know so little about world affairs and other cultures

➤ What American students learn in school at home

➤ How holidays such as Thanksgiving and Halloween are celebrated

➤ Living standards at home

➤ The misconception that all Americans own guns and that random violence is a fact of everyday life

✳ DIVERSITY

✈ How mixed populations get along at home

✈ How different regions of the country relate to one another

✳ FAST FOOD AND DIET

✈ How American products such as Coca-Cola™ and McDonalds™ are marketed

✈ How Americans typically eat and how the obesity epidemic has come about

✈ Questions about the fascination with peanut butter and jelly sandwiches for children

Naturally, you can't be expected to have all of the answers to all of the questions. Just make sure to educate yourself before you go so you can speak intelligently on topics that are likely to arise. Above all, make sure you don't let any anti-American sentiments discourage you from exploring your host country to the fullest.

Also, remember that host nationals around the world tend to question the activities of the U.S. government, whether in a time of peace or of crisis. So no matter when you go abroad, you'll want to be prepared: Use common sense, keep a low profile, dress to blend in, and avoid overt displays of American patriotism.

NSCS TAKE-ABROADS

✈ Anti-American sentiments exist on all parts of the globe. Be aware of them, but don't take them personally. Generally, those sentiments are directed toward the government.

✈ You may find that people in your host country know as much about American news as you do. Keep current on the news back home so you can have an educated conversation.

✈ The Internet is the main source exchange students use to keep up with current news.

✈ Breaking stereotypes is one of your jobs as an exchange student.

CHAPTER

10

Returning Home

"There is nothing left of our journey, except for the memories and photographs. But it has been so much more than a journey. It has been everything that had been missing in my life. I will be utterly alone again, yet this time I will walk with confidence, unafraid of the unknown. I will not be that same country boy who had been suffocating in Kansas, waiting for a chance to experience life. I have lived it; I have done it. I will walk through the streets of my life looking for every chance to experience something new. The world I live in is exactly the same, but the man is different."

Jason O.
Hays, KS
Fort Hays State University

5¢

Few people prepare for their return home, because they expect it to be easy; however, many are surprised when it is not. In fact, dealing with this part of the overseas study experience is often overlooked. So much of you will have changed while you were away: new routines, tastes, ideas, perhaps even values. And now your job is to integrate all of that back into your life at home. This isn't an easy task.

Several factors determine how stressful your transition will be. Naturally, the longer you have been away, the harder your return will probably be. The degree of cultural difference between your home and host cultures will play a role as well. In other words, returning from Sweden or Australia will be far different from returning from Indonesia or Ghana. And how much communication you had with friends and family back home over the duration will make a difference, as well.

WHAT WILL IT BE LIKE TO RETURN HOME AFTER SO LONG?

Coming home from study abroad can be difficult, but it can also be when you learn the most from your cross-cultural experience. Usually, it takes a while to realize the true impact of study abroad. After all, you have had an experience on many levels.

Reverse culture shock usually takes students by surprise, but it is a very real part of the return home. It will probably take a bit of time before you begin to feel entirely comfortable in your surroundings again, no matter how familiar they may seem. Many students feel culture shock far more upon their return home than upon their arrival in their host country. A once-familiar home culture can seem so unfamiliar that it takes some time to readjust.

During reverse culture shock, you may experience the following:

✈ The sensation that you're out of place even though you are home

✈ The realization that others aren't interested in hearing about your adventures in too much detail

✈ The feeling that you are bored or restless with life at home

✈ The realization that relationships with family and friends have changed

✈ The impression that others misunderstand the ways in which you have changed

✈ The inclination to judge your home culture and country in a critical way

Some NSCS students are thrilled to return home, and some are saddened, but the majority have bittersweet emotions. Mostly, the feeling is about a sense of loss: loss of using another language, loss of being challenged by living overseas, and loss of experiencing the everyday adventures of communicating cross-culturally. Communicating to your friends and family all that you have experienced and learned will be important to you, but you'll probably also want to stay connected to your host culture and friends overseas.

You are likely to feel conflicted emotions for a few days, weeks, or even months until you readjust to your home environment. You have just returned home with an expanded view of the world, and you have had so many new experiences. But you're also likely to feel a little out of place: You might feel disoriented, not knowing if the words you are using are those of your home or host country. And you might feel as though you are dreaming or that life has taken on a surreal quality.

It's also common for students who have spent time abroad to become rather negative about American society: It's too superficial, too consumerist, too fast. You might withdraw and feel out of place. But be assured that with time, you'll be able to blend what you have learned overseas with what you have built up at home.

Students found that they had missed the following from back home:

✈ Significant others

✈ Family

✈ American food that wasn't available in the host country (pizza, hamburgers, French fries)

✈ Smoke-free environments

✈ Ice

✈ Their own beds

✈ English

✈ Fast Internet connections

✈ Hot water

✈ Freedoms of country/government

✈ Air-conditioning

However, upon arriving home, students missed the following from their host countries:

- ✈ More free time

- ✈ Easier classes

- ✈ Using a foreign language

- ✈ Exploring new places

- ✈ Walking everywhere

- ✈ Efficient public transportation

- ✈ Being surrounded by so much history

- ✈ Dancing like a native

- ✈ Outdoor cafés

- ✈ Landscape and scenery

- ✈ Being treated like an adult (less age restrictions)

After the "honeymoon" phase of your return concludes, you might see things about your own culture a bit more clearly and objectively—just as an outsider would.

Here are a few negative stereotypes that some students found to be true of Americans upon their return home:

- ✈ Excessive amount of choices in the grocery stores

- ✈ The fast pace of life

- ✈ The large size of homes and rooms

- ✈ Materialism and excessive use of resources

- ✈ Obesity

- ✈ The fact that making money seems more important than enjoying life

- ✈ An undefined "culture" in the United States

- ✈ Superficial friendships

"On the one hand, I cannot wait to get home to eat steak, sit on a real toilet, play with my dog, and hug my family. On the other hand, I do not want to leave Uganda because of the two Ugandan families that have sheltered me, a total stranger. They have cooked for me, invited me to their table to eat, helped me adjust to the culture, shared their faith and friends, walked me through the town, and patiently listened to my endless stories about life in America.

I just need to be able to cry to someone or yell or look at all my pictures and escape into the goodness that each photograph captures. How do I describe all I have seen to my friends back in America? How do I explain how Ronny, a staff member at the local nongovernmental organization, has taken me under his care, or how do I retell Dr. Arthur's amazing stories? How do you explain the peace of a sunset or the stench of poverty? How do you not cry when you look back at the pictures of smiling children who are now dead from preventable diseases like malaria?

How does my experience in Uganda impact my life? I am not who I was three months ago. Will my family and friends understand? I do not want to be in Uganda anymore, but I am not sure I want to be home, either."

Amber H.
Ames, IA
Iowa State University

Although these stereotypes were tough for students to accept, the new knowledge helped them to be more insightful. Coupled with the positive stereotypes that had been reinforced while abroad (such as the friendliness of Americans), they were able to have a renewed, yet realistic, pride in their culture.

HOW CAN YOU TRANSITION BACK TO LIFE AT HOME?

Upon your return home, you will also adjust back to the American pace of life: typical modes of transportation, being able to respond in English without giving it a second thought (unlike learning a second language), accents, size of your room, food, what "on time" really means, and driving on the right side of the road, among others. But more significant will be the more life-changing adjustments, such as how you view the world's resources, materialism, or wealth in the United States. At the very least, you will be more mature and more globally aware.

Some returning students say relationships with family and friends are the most difficult aspects of returning home. You may find that people aren't particularly interested in hearing your stories after the initial welcome. It's common to want to talk about your own affairs. This may make you feel like an outsider. All of a sudden, your home environment doesn't measure up to that ideal mental image you held before you got on the plane home.

Don't put pressure on yourself to readjust back home too quickly. Withhold self-judgment, a strict timeline, and unrealistic expectations. You have undergone major changes by living overseas and shouldn't be surprised if you need to sleep a little more, cry a little more, or journal a little more. You also might have missed a good deal of events and stories while you were away, and you are likely to feel a disconnect when people speak about them. You may feel that you're the only one who has changed and that everything else has remained the same.

To ease your transition, doing the following might help:

→ Express your feelings with those you love and ask for a little space.

→ Share some stories of time overseas but hold back the most interesting stories and tell them over time.

→ Remember that your return is also difficult on your family and friends, who likely see a change in you.

→ Give yourself time to readjust.

NSCS students tell us that for the most part, their friends and family members wanted to hear about their travels but only for so long. Sending photos or group letters via email can be useful, as people can review these in their own time.

HOW CAN YOU KEEP THE EXPERIENCE ALIVE?

Some NSCS students found that once they returned home, they felt closer to their new friends overseas and fellow exchange students than to friends they had known for years. These can be important and rewarding connections: You shared a lot with these people, and continuing these friendships will be important, even as you pick up your life at home. About half of all NSCS students stay in touch with their new friends abroad.

Recounting memories alone is also a great way to remind yourself of all that you have experienced. NSCS students advise you to do the following things.

✳ WHILE YOU ARE OVERSEAS

✈ Make a travel journal (in your host country language).

✈ Draw pictures of the landscape or architecture.

✈ Collect something from every country you visit.

✈ Save ticket stubs of attractions, playbills, and flyers.

✈ Make notes in a calendar so you record the exact day of each event.

✈ Buy postcards of the places you can't photograph or to get higher quality pictures.

✈ Jot down phrases and quotes that you hear.

✈ Keep a map of each city you visit.

✈ Make sure you say a proper good-bye (and even give a small gift) to those whom you got to know well, and be sure to exchange contact information.

✳ ONCE YOU ARRIVE HOME

✈ Be realistic about having some catching up to do on things that happened while you were away.

✈ Share your stories with your study abroad office for their use in brochures or fairs, or offer to speak with prospective study abroad students.

✈ Set up a blog.

✈ Write a story or essay about your experiences (check out glimpsefoundation.org or transitionsabroad.com).

✈ Make a PowerPoint presentation of your top memories.

✈ Retell your stories so they are fresh in your memory.

✈ Turn your photos into a scrapbook or CD.

✈ Exchange your pictures with friends from your program so that you have twice as many.

✈ Save your emails as a journal.

✈ Keep in touch with friends overseas who will help you remember.

✈ Write articles for your school or local newspaper about your experience.

✈ Seek out situations in which international experiences and perspectives are appreciated.

Studying abroad is designed to give you a taste of the world that's out there, and the result is often a thirst for travel and adventure. Many study abroad students go on to travel extensively or even work overseas. By living in a foreign country, you have faced yourself in a different sort of way: You have proven that you have the confidence to succeed in a different environment.

NSCS TAKE-ABROADS

✈ Reverse culture shock is real and should be expected, so give yourself time to readjust to home.

✈ You might find that returning is bittersweet. You are missing some elements of overseas but are happy to have some elements of your home country back, too.

✈ You will be able to see your own home culture more objectively, appreciating both the positive and the negative aspects.

✈ Your friends and family most likely will want to hear your stories, but you will need to find other outlets for sharing or remembering your time overseas.

✈ There are myriad ways to remember your overseas memories. Find the one that works for you so you have a tangible product to keep forever.

✈ On a more practical note, find out when and how your courses from abroad are recorded onto your transcripts at home.

CHAPTER

11

More Postcards and Letters from Abroad

"Frankly, before I left for Africa I had no idea what I was getting myself into! I was excited, anxious, tired, and felt insecure and confident all at the same time. My goal was to take one day at a time and allow myself time to process all my experiences. When I arrived I found out that Africa renews and challenges the body and mind. My fears of bugs and snakes quickly dissipated so I could tackle greater challenges and obstacles— like how to prevent children from dying of hunger."

Amber H.
Ames, IA
Iowa State University

"During my time in Seville, Spain, I volunteered teaching English in a high school. For half of the time, I worked with a class of thirteen-year-olds, and for the other half I worked with professors who wanted to learn English. The kids were fun because they were so excited to attempt to speak English, and although they didn't know many words, all the boys made sure to ask me in perfect English, 'Do you have a boyfriend?' Working with the professors was also a blast because they were delightfully warm and welcoming and so incredibly enthusiastic to try out their English skills.

I also agreed to help at an *alojamiento* (tourism) class, which is similar to vocational schools in the States. My experience there was quite different than my time in the high school. Professor Jesus led me in front of a class and informed the students that I would be teaching them critical phrases in English, and then he just left me there alone, standing in front of the class, with chalk in my hand and sweat trickling down my forehead. I immediately blurted out, 'I don't know what I got myself into!' and the students laughed and looked at me without having the slightest idea of what I said. It ended up going very smoothly and I left that night thinking, 'I was just a substitute for a tourism class full of students my age or older in Spain, without being prepared, or even knowing I would be teaching.' Quite random, but I managed to pull it off!

My time in Spain has allowed me to express myself better and to overcome my fears without avoiding situations. My usual tendency to worry too much was often pushed aside because everything was out of the blue. Normally, if I had known that I was going to be teaching a class, I would have been a frazzled wreck, and may have even avoided the opportunity altogether. Instead, I was relaxed going into it, and when the situation unraveled, I dealt with it and it ended up not being so bad. I learned to give myself more credit and not underestimate my capabilities. Thus, I can push myself to take risks and excel in the future...and I can actually speak Spanish now!"

Katherine Ely
St. Charles, IN
Indiana University

"The first part of my planned weekend journey, as always, was actually getting to the destination, which was Kiev. I had scoured the Internet for weeks trying to find the cheapest and quickest flight from Prague, and turned up nothing but discouraging results. One site would declare the price to be $200, only for it to turn to $410 after the "taxes and fees" were added at checkout time. All offered to first send me through various locations around Europe: Vienna, Warsaw, Frankfurt.

Largely out of curiosity, I decided to visit a travel agency and see what kind of options they gave me. It is there that I discovered there were, in fact, direct flights from Prague to Kiev, and they were decently priced as well. Apparently Czech Airlines decided to only let their travel agent partners in on this little secret. Let this be a lesson and a warning: Just because you can't find a flight online doesn't mean it doesn't exist; you just have to really go looking for it."

Dmitriy Zakharov
Mobile, AL
Georgetown University

More Postcards and Letters from Abroad ❂ 193

"The story of the 3,000 detenidos-desaparecidos—the detained and disappeared—is not as well known as it should be. Between 1973 and 1990, much of the Chilean population suffered under the dictatorial regime of General Augusto Pinochet, who kidnapped and murdered scores of political prisoners accused of being Communist sympathizers. Many of these atrocities occurred at Villa Grimaldi, a former prison camp which has since been transformed into a park memorial to those persecuted there during the Pinochet regime.

On the day I decided to visit the park, I met an elderly male survivor of the regime's persecution. As we walked, he struggled to speak, releasing his words only as they came to him as he recalled the horrors he endured. He pointed out where prisoners had been hung by their feet, submerged in freezing water, locked in narrow closets, and subjected to boiling water poured over their bodies—all due to an anti-Communist paranoia, a saturating fear of those who thought differently than was officially accepted.

The most surreal part of the experience, however, was not in learning about the atrocities that occurred at Villa Grimaldi, but rather the conversation that followed with my host mother. I rushed into the kitchen, eager to discuss my day's experience with a Chilean, who had lived through this tainted period herself. I was not prepared, however, for the look of anger and disbelief on her face when I told her where I had been that day.

"Do you know what it was like to have to stand in line, hoping that I would be rationed enough milk to feed my babies?" she asked, recalling her life under the Socialist leader Salvador Allende, who was deposed by Pinochet.

Though I found it shocking that she could so easily deny the existence of a torture camp so close to her own home, I found her point of view is shared by a significant percentage of Chileans. She had suffered considerably under the Socialist system, and her explanation prevented me from leaving Chile with a biased opinion toward the past. While I did not agree with her, her comments represented the harsh duality of the Chilean national memory. I left that conversation with my host mother immersed in both sides of the story."

Samantha Friedman
Mobile, AL
Georgetown University

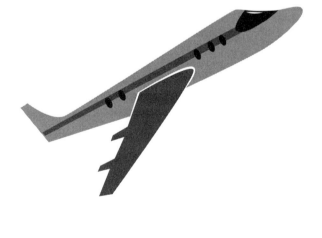

APPENDIX

1

General Advice for Family Members

Getting support at home can be complex if family members don't share your enthusiasm for study abroad. NSCS students have some advice for parents or family members who want to be supportive, but just don't know how to go about it:

- ✈ Be positive, but don't be afraid to ask about the details: cost, accommodation, how credits will transfer.

- ✈ Help your child plan a budget to make sure the plan is realistic.

- ✈ Don't focus solely on money issues. Remember that plenty of scholarship money is available.

- ✈ Be available. Let him know you care and are willing to let him try new things.

- ✈ Be a good listener. Then you'll be understood.

- ✈ Ask a lot of questions. It will help him in the decision-making process.

✈ Outline all the dangers that may be associated with a foreign country, without scaring your child into not wanting to go.

✈ Don't pressure your child about her choice of country, but help with the research if you're asked.

✈ Consider the inspirations your child has and choose a country that will accommodate those inspirations yet also provide safety.

✈ Don't downplay how difficult the trip will be for your child and your family as well.

✈ Don't get too involved. The whole point is for your child to become more independent.

✈ Speak with the professor who is organizing the trip if you are hesitant or concerned about your child's safety.

✈ Do your own research. Buy a travel book and read the news from that country to be better involved.

✈ Buy your child a mini language dictionary for traveling, and practice phrases with him regularly.

✈ Don't forget that you'll be able to communicate with your child while she's abroad, just not as easily, as often, or as cheaply.

✈ Buy an international phone card and figure out how to use it together.

✈ Write lots of letters or emails once she goes.

✈ Visit your child at the end of the program. You'll be amazed at how much he will have learned!

✈ Listen to her stories, even if you're tired of hearing them. Don't roll your eyes or mutter, "Oh no, not again." The student who has just finished studying abroad might be a very different student from the one who left.

REGRETS AND DO-OVERS?

When asked if there was anything they would have done differently if given the chance, most NSCS students said they would have would have stayed longer, traveled more, and made more friends among the local population.

Beyond these top responses, they also wish they had done the following:

✈ Been more outgoing with locals

✈ Used open-ended tickets

✈ Taken more pictures

✈ Looked into other program options and compared more

✈ Budgeted more effectively

✈ Kept a journal

✈ Gone to a more exotic country

✈ Saved more money beforehand so they could have taken more weekend trips

✈ Gone earlier and taken language classes

✈ Lived with native speakers

✈ Kept their valuables in a money pouch

✈ Volunteered

✈ Realized it would be hard in the beginning and been okay with that

EXPECTATIONS FULFILLED?

When asked if anything was different in reality from what they had imagined, NSCS students responded that, for the most part, everything was different!

Things they didn't expect to experience (but in fact did) were the following:

- ✈ Finding it hard to communicate with family and friends

- ✈ Enjoying the native food

- ✈ Getting attention and stares from locals

- ✈ Making such great friends

- ✈ Dealing with frequent travel delays on mass transportation

✈ Living so remotely

✈ Spending so much money

✈ Hearing so much English

✈ Receiving more one-on-one help with classes

✈ Dispelling stereotypes about their host culture

✈ Feeling comfortable in a faraway place

✈ Experiencing more anti-American sentiment

✈ Witnessing different colors in the landscape

✈ Doing laundry by hand

✈ Finding so many similarities to the culture at home

APPENDIX

2

Resources for Planning an Adventure Abroad

The following resources* are extremely useful for anyone interested in travel and/or study abroad.

✳ BOOKS

Bracht	Lonely Planet
Fodor's	Rick Steves
Frommer's	Rough Guide
Let's Go	Time Out

✳ ORGANIZATIONS

✈ Council on Standards for International Education Travel: www.csiet.org

✈ Forum on Education Abroad: www.forumea.org

*Note: These listings are for information and exploration purposes only. While several of these organizations are strategic partners with NSCS, we neither endorse nor receive compensation for providing these as recommended resources.

※ INTERNSHIP PROGRAMS FOR STUDY ABROAD STUDENTS

✦ Academic Year in America, High School Foreign Exchange Programs: academicyear.org

✦ American Institute for Foreign Study: aifs.com

✦ Association for International Practical Training: aipt.org

✦ (CDS) International: *http://cdsintl.org*

✦ University of California—Irvine, Center for International Education: www.cie.uci.edu

✦ Foundation for Sustainable Development: fsdinternational.org

✦ German Academic Exchange Service: daad.org

✦ Global Service Corps: globalservicecorps.org

- ✈ Idealist.org: Action Without Borders: www.idealist.org

- ✈ Intern Abroad: www.internabroad.com

- ✈ International Association for the Exchange of Students for Technical Experience: www.iaeste.org

- ✈ International Service Learning: islonline.org

- ✈ Michigan State University, International Studies & Programs: isp.msu.edu

- ✈ International Studies Abroad: www.studyabroaddirectory.com

- ✈ StudyAbroad.com

- ✈ Transitions Abroad: transitionsabroad.com

- ✈ University of Minnesota: Learning Abroad Center: umabroad.umn.edu

✳ INFORMATION FOR STUDENTS WITH DISABILITIES

➤ *Americans with Disabilities Act*: ada.gov

➤ Mobility International USA: www.miusa.org

✳ EDUCATION

➤ ACCENT International Consortium for Academic Programs Abroad: accentintl.com

➤ (AFS) Intercultural Programs: afs.org

➤ Alliance Abroad Group: allianceabroad.com

➤ AmeriSpan, The Bridge Between Cultures: amerispan.com

➤ Association of International Educators (NAFSA): nafsa.org

➤ Blue Ventures: blueventures.org

➤ British American Educational Foundation: baef.org

➤ British Council: www.britishcouncil.org

- Center for Global Education, Worldwide Colleges and Universities: globaled.us/wwcu

- Institute of International Education: iie.org

- International Partnership for Service-Learning and Leadership: ipsl.org

- International Scholar Laureate Program: www.scholarlaureate.org

- Nacel Open Door: nacelopendoor.org

- National Society for Experiential Education: nsee.org

- The Scholar Ship: thescholarship.com

- School for International Training: sit.edu

- SEAmester Program (University of Massachusetts—Dartmouth): www.umassd.edu/seamester

- Semester at Sea: semesteratsea.com

- United Nations Educational, Scientific, and Cultural Organization: portal.unesco.org

- Up with People: upwithpeople.org

✳ VOLUNTEER

✈ City Year: www.cityyear.org

✈ Cross-Cultural Solutions: crossculturalsolutions.org

✈ Foundation for Sustainable Development: fsdinternational.org

✈ Global Citizens Network: globalcitizens.org

✈ Global Crossroad: globalcrossroad.com

✈ Global Routes: globalroutes.org

✈ Global Service Corps: globalservicecorps.org

✈ Global Vision International: gvi.co.uk

✈ Global Volunteers Network: volunteer.org.nz

✈ i-to-i: i-to-i.com

✈ International Volunteer Program: ivpsf.org

✈ International Volunteer Programs Association: www.volunteerinternational.org

✈ Madventurer: madventurer.com

✈ Operation Crossroads Africa: operationcrossroadsafrica.org

✈ Peace Corps: www.peacecorps.gov

✈ Projects Abroad: projects-abroad.org

✈ RTPnet: rtpnet.org

✈ Students Partnership Worldwide: spw.org

✈ Volunteers for Peace, International Voluntary Service: vfp.org

✈ WorldTeach: worldteach.org

✈ World Volunteer Web: worldvolunteerweb.org

WORK AND TEACH

- Alliance Abroad Group: allianceabroad.com

- British Universities North America Club:
  www.bunac.org

- Council on International Educational Exchange:
  ciee.org

- GoAbroad.com: www.goabroad.com

- Interexchange: interexchange.org

CUSTOMS

- How Stuff Works:
  travel.howstuffworks.com/customs.htm

- U.S. Customs and Border Protection:
  www.customs.ustreas.gov

✳ TRAVEL AND CULTURAL GUIDES

✈ Central Intelligence Agency, World Factbook:
www.cia.gov/cia/publications/factbook/index.html

✈ CultureGrams: culturegrams.com

✈ Europe: A Never-Ending Journey:
www.visiteurope.com

✈ Europe from a Backpack: europebackpack.com

✈ Fodor's Travel Guides: fodors.com

✈ Frommer's Travel Guides: frommers.com

✈ Intercultural Press: www.interculturalpress.com

✈ Let's Go Travel Guides: www.letsgo.com

✈ Lonely Planet: www.lonelyplanet.com

✈ Michigan State University Global Access:
msuglobalaccess.net

✈ Rough Guides: roughguides.com

✈ wGuides: wguides.com

✈ World 66 Travel Guide: world66.com

Resources for Planning an Adventure Abroad   ✿   213

✳ EMBASSIES

✈ Electronic Embassy Website: embassy.org

✈ Embassyworld.com

✳ HOSTELS

✈ Hostelling International: hihostels.com

✈ Hostels of Europe, The Independent Hostel Network: www.hostelseurope.com

✈ Hostels.com: www.hostels.com

✈ Hostelworld: hostelworld.com

✈ Hostelz.com: www.hostelz.com

✳ TRAVEL

✈ Worldwide Bicycle Tour Directory: bicycletour.com

✈ Eurail: www.eurail.com

✈ Eurostar: www.eurostar.com

✈ Rail Europe, Your European Travel Experts:
www.raileurope.com

✈ Rick Steves' Europe: ricksteves.com

✈ Routes International Travel Services:
routesinternational.com

✈ STA Travel (cheap student airfare and hotels):
www.statravel.com

✈ Trail Database: traildatabase.org

✈ Walkingworld (UK walking guide):
walkingworld.com

✈ Dan Youra Studios World Ferries:
youra.com/intlferries/index.html

✳ STUDENT AID AND SCHOLARSHIPS

✈ Alexander von Humboldt Foundation:
www.humboldt-foundation.de

✈ FastWeb; Scholarships, Financial Aid, and Colleges:
fastweb.com

✈ Federal Student Aid, Student Aid on the Web:
studentaid.ed.gov

✈ FinAid! SmartStudent Guide to Financial Aid:
finaid.com

✈ Free Application for Federal Student Aid (FAFSA):
www.fafsa.ed.gov

✈ Fulbright Scholar Program: www.cies.org/cies.htm

✈ International Education Finance Corporation:
iefc.com

✈ International Education Financial Aid: iefa.org

✈ NSCS Scholar Abroad Scholarship Program:
nscs.org/scholarships/scholarabroad.cfm

✈ Rhodes Scholarships: rhodesscholar.org

✈ Worldstudy.gov Boren Awards: worldstudy.gov

✴ HEALTH AND SAFETY

✈ Association for Safe International Road Travel:
asirt.org

✈ Centers for Disease Control, Travelers' Health:
www.cdc.gov/travel/index.htm

✈ Health Awareness Connection: healthac.org

✈ No Nonsense Self-Defense: nononsenseselfdefense.com

✈ The Roofie Foundation: roofie.com

✈ Travel Health Online: www.tripprep.com

✈ U.S. Department of Health and Human Services:
www.globalhealth.gov

✈ U.S. Department of Homeland Security:
www.ready.gov

✈ U.S. Department of State, Travel Warnings and
Consular Information Sheets:
travel.state.gov/travel/cis_pa_tw/cis_pa_tw_1168.html

✳ THINGS YOU NEED TO KNOW ABOUT THE LAW

➶ U.S. Department of State, Bureau of Educational and Cultural Affairs: exchanges.state.gov

➶ U.S. Department of State, Law & Policy: travel.state.gov/law/

➶ World Legal Information Institute: worldlii.org

✳ EMERGENCY TRAVEL INFORMATION

➶ Assist America Global Emergency Services: assistamerica.com

➶ InsureMyTrip.com

✳ IDENTIFICATION

➶ International Student Identification Cards: isecard.com

➶ Travel Document Systems: traveldocs.com

➶ U.S. Department of State,Document Requirements: travel.state.gov/travel/cis_pa_tw/cis_pa_tw_1168.html

218   ✪   Adventures Abroad

Index

A

Academic study abroad offices, 53
Adjustments, 57–83
    see also Returning home
    advice, 75
    communication barriers, 58–60
    host country friends, 76
    immersing yourself, 66–73
Adventure, desire for, 3
Advice/advisors, 12–13
Africa, 191. *See also* specific country
Agbaje, Esther, 145
Airline flights/fares, 193
Alcohol use, 73, 123
Allende, Salvador, 195
AltaVista's Babel Fish, 63
Ambassadorship, 164–69
    countering anti-Americanism,
        167–69
    dealing with anti-Americanism,
        164–65
    experiencing stereotyping, 166
"American scene," 118
Anti-American sentiment, 155, 164–69
    countering, 167–69
    dealing with, 164–65
Argentina, 95, 131
Arrogance, 118, 170
Asia. *See* specific country
Assignments, clarifying, 103
ATM machines, 158
Attitude, 69
Au pairs, 52
Australia, 95, 150
Austria, 122, 124

B

Babel Fish, 63
Bargaining, 59
Beer, 123

Belize, 91
Bias, 168, 194
Blogging, 37, 55, 188
Body language
    gesturing, 80
    personal interactions and, 71, 77
    volume of speech, 78
Books (resources), 205
Bragin, Paul, 107
Breucker, Kendra, 10
Budgeting side trips, 115
Buenos Aires, Argentina, 131
Business offices overseas, 52

C

Cameras, digital, 35
Campus resources, 12–13, 17
Cape Town, South Africa, 67, 133, 145
Cell phones, 37
Centers for Disease Control, 25
Chat rooms, 37
Chile, 77, 96, 195
China, 80, 93
City layouts, 111
Classroom experience
    essay questions, 93
    expectations of professors, 89–92
    grades, 91, 94, 100–101
    homework deadlines, 92
    language barriers, 102–4, 105
    minimizing obstacles, 99
    NSCS student observations, 94–99
    obstacles faced by NSCS students,
        97–98
    personalized attention, 93
    readings and study time, 92, 102
    uniqueness of, 86–88
Cleary, Alison, 127
Closeness and touching, 155
Colombia, 95

Comfort level/comfort zone, 4, 5, 110, 132, 159
Communication, 34–37, 41
   barriers, 58–60
   cell phones with international calling plans, 37
   digital cameras, 35
   e-mail, 34
   "face" giving, 59–60
   family visits, 36
   in foreign language, 63
   homesickness and, 38
   with host family prior to arriving, 39
   international phone cards, 34
   Internet chat rooms/IMs/blogging, 37
   Internet phone service, 35
   letters and postcards, 35
   nonverbal, 58, 59
   parental advice, 199
   with strangers, 71, 134
   surprise gifts prior to departure, 36
   webcams and microphones, 36
Community service, 53
Compliments, giving and receiving, 59
Connectedness. See Communication
Contact lenses, 28
Conversation groups, 76
Costa Rica, 91, 93
Country choice. See Destination, choosing
Course work
   changing, 104
   class participation, 105
   study time, 102
Credit cards, 22
Credits, transferring, 100–101, 105, 190
Crime, 150–52
Cross-cultural perceptions, 73
Cultural appeal, 2–3
Cultural beliefs, 58
Cultural differences, in classroom, 86–87, 89, 90, 105
Cultural guides, 213
Cultural preferences, 91
Cultural values, 39
Culture, American, 170–72
Curfew, 113
Currency, understanding, 156
Customs, 212
Cyprus, 95

Czech cuisine, 65
Czech Republic, 88, 142

D
Daily schedule, 68
Dating, 81
Debating skills, 145
Debit cards, 22
Deferring college admission, 48, 49, 56
Denmark, 95
Dental checkup, 28
Destination, choosing, 4–10, 17
   economic considerations, 4
   immunizations and, 27
   language skills and, 4
   logistical considerations, 6
   main factors, 7
   NSCS student choices, 9
   personal connections, 8
   programs offered, 7
Dictionaries, 63, 103, 201
Digital cameras, 35
Diphtheria, 27
Directions, when exploring, 110
Disabled students, 208
Diversity, 172
Documentation and paperwork, 19–22, 157
   following specific instructions, 21
   of immunizations, 27
   making copies of, 21
   passports and visas, 19–20
   starting the process, 21, 41
Domestic helpers, 52
Do-overs, 200–201

E
Eating. See Food and eating
Ecuador, 79, 96
Edmonson, Elayne, 5
Education resources, 208–9
Elephanta Island (India), 127
Ely, Katherine, 192
E-mail, 34
Embassies, 156, 214
Emergency fund, 24
Emergency travel information, 218
Emotional motivation, 4
Employment experience. See Internship programs

220 ✪ Index

England, 77, 81, 92, 95, 123
English language, 60
Essay questions, 93
Ethnocentric viewpoints, 69
Etiquette, 73, 124
Expectations, 202–3
Expenses and funding
    credit and debit cards, 22
    emergency fund, 24
    for exploring, 108
    financial assistance/scholarships,
        23–24
    for gap year, 51
    gifts, 24
    resourcefulness and, 41
    resources, 216
    scholarships, 216
    spending money, 24
Exploring, 107–30
    advice, 117–18
    alone *versus* group, 111
    city layouts, 111
    etiquette, 124
    food and eating out, 120–26, 130
    free time, 128
    getting directions, 110
    local scheduling and, 112
    logistical challenges, 113–14
    money and, 108
    personal and sociological, 119, 130
    prioritizing, 115–16
    safety and, 112
    travel style and, 108
    weekend getaway ideas, 129
Eye contact, 79
Eye examination, 28

F
"Face" giving, 59–60
Family support, 3–4, 17, 197–203
Family visits, 36
Fast food, 171, 172
Financing. *See* Expenses and funding
First aid kit, 28
Flirting, 158
Florence, Italy, 85
Focus, 117
Food and eating, 120–26, 130
    adjusting to, 66, 120
    cultural differences, 126

customer service/tipping, 125
Czech, 65
duration/timing of meals, 121
fast food, 171, 172
meal preparation/ingredients, 123
mealtimes, 121
special diets, 125
Foot positioning, 80
Foreign currency, 156
Foreign newspapers, 52
Formality, 81–82
France, 79, 81, 91, 92, 93, 95, 123, 124
Friedman, Samantha, 195
Friends
accompanied by, 11, 17
from host country, 76, 103, 134, 186
Funding. *See* Expenses and funding

G
Gandhi, Mohandas (Mahatma Gandhi),
    136
Gap year, 43–56
    benefits, 50
    considerations, 46
    defined, 44–45
    job interviews afterwards, 54
    making the most of, 47–50
    planning, 50–53, 56
    purposefulness in, 45, 53
    sharing experience of, 55
Gender relations/role differences, 72
Germany, 90, 92, 95, 124
Gesturing, 80
Gifts, surprise, 36
Gilman Scholarship, 13
Giving "face," 59–60
Glasses (eye glasses), 28
Going alone, 11
Greece, 91, 95
Group travel, 111, 116

H
Hand gestures, 80
Hartnett, Rebekah, 67, 133
Head shaking and nodding, 80
Health considerations, 25–32
    dental and eye exams, 28
    health and safety resources, 217
    immunizations, 25, 27
    medical checkup, 25

Index   221

medications, 28
preparedness, 41
Hepatitis (A and B), 27
Home, clinging to, 134
Homesickness, 38, 40
Home stay. *See* Host families
Homework, 92
Hong Kong, 96
Hostels, 214
Host families, 14–16
    communicating with, 60
    friendships and, 76
    meeting, 57
Hugging, 77
Humbleness, 194
Humility, 59, 78
Hungary, 79

I
Identification, 218
Immersion
    in culture, 132–38, 147
    in language, 1, 55, 64
Immunizations, 25, 27
India, 80, 127
Instant messages, 37
Intercambios, 76
International calling plans, 37
International exchange students, 47
International phone cards, 34, 199
Internet
    chat rooms, 37
    as news source, 173
Internship programs, 139–43, 206–7
    benefits, 140–41
    stipends/travel benefits, 143
Invitations, 135
Ireland, 91, 93, 96
Italy, 77, 80, 85, 90, 93, 94, 96, 107

J
Jaisalmere, India, 127
Japan, 8, 79, 90, 91, 96, 150
Job interviews, 54
Jodhpur, India, 127
Jordan, 80, 91

K
Kiev, Ukraine, 70, 153, 193
Kissing, 77

L
Language(s)
    classroom issues and, 87
    dictionaries, 63, 103, 201
    English, 60
    immersion, 1, 55, 64
    nonverbal, 71
    patience with, 104
    practicing, 58–59
    Spanish, 58
    tonal, 58
    Latin America, 78. *See also* specific
        country
Laughter, 135
Law enforcement, 64, 154, 158
Legal resources, 218
Living accommodations, 14–16
Loeswick, Megan, 85
London, England, 109
"Loud American" stereotype, 78

M
Madrid, Spain, 16
Malaria, 27
Marzullo, Emily, 40, 169
Mealtimes, 121. *See also* Food and eating
Medications, 28
Merit-based scholarships, 23
Mexico, 77, 94, 96
Molidina, Mehreen, 109
Money, understanding, 156
Morals, 118
Movies, 171
Mumbai, India, 127
Music groups, 76

N
Native families, 17
Nemiroff, Russell, 16
Netherlands, The, 96
Networking groups, 76
New experiences, 135
New Zealand, 92, 95
Nodding, 80
Nonverbal communication, 58, 59

O
Olomouc, Czech Republic, 88
Open-mindedness, 1
Organizations (resources), 205

Organized clubs, 76
Ortiz, Robin, 136

P

Pace, 78
Packaged trips, 116
Palacky University (Czech Republic), 88
Paperwork. *See* Documentation and paperwork
Passport, 19–20
Peace Corps, 7
Perceptions, cross-cultural, 73
Personal hygiene, 28, 71
Personality, 71
Personal proximity/space, 77
Perspectives, 3
Peru, 96
Phone cards, international, 34, 199
Photography, 35
Pickpockets, 152, 161
Pinochet, Augusto, 195
Planning
    gap year, 50–53, 56
    resources, 205–18
Poland, 123
Police, 64, 154, 158
Policies, U.S., 165
Politics, world
    demonstrations, 155, 159
    monitoring conditions, 156
    questions asked of students, 170
Poplawski, Paulina, 88
Prague, Czech Republic, 142
Preconceived notions, 7
Public transportation, 67, 69, 108, 112, 113, 159

R

Reasons, for overseas study, 2–4
Regrets, 200-201
Religious sites, 114
Research, 53
Resources, home campus, 12–13, 17
Rest, 119
Resume, 140
Returning home, 175–90
    expressing yourself, 188–89
    keeping the experience alive, 186–89
    missing host country, 181

negative American stereotypes, 182, 184
    reverse culture shock, 177–79, 190
    transitioning, 184–85
    to what was missed, 180
Reverse culture shock. *See under* Returning home
Rome, Italy, 107
Russia, 79

S

Safety, 149–61
    advice, 157–60
    anti-American sentiment, 155
    awareness of surroundings, 149, 151, 161
    closeness and touching, 155
    crime, 150–52
    crossing the street, 113
    documents and, 157
    instincts and, 154
    local law enforcement, 154
    planning to get home (to dorm/house etc.), 154, 158
    proactive approach to, 161
    resources, 217
    when exploring, 112
Same-sex interactions, 72
Scheduling, 112, 115
Scholarships, 23–24, 216
Scotland, 92
Security, 150. *See also* Safety
Self-awareness, 45, 56
Self-discipline, 92
Self-knowledge, 3
Seville, Spain, 10, 61, 192
Shoes, 114
Singburi, Thailand, 136
Single traveling, 11
Skype, 35
Smiling, 79
Social interaction
    formality, 81-82
    gesturing, 80
    personal proximity, 77
    smiling, 79
    speed of life, 78
    volume of speech, 78
South Africa, 96
South America. *See* specific country

Index ❂ 223

Spain, 10, 16, 61, 78, 90, 92, 96, 124, 192
Spanish language, 58
Spending money, 24
Spontaneity, 135
Sports groups, 76
Stereotypes
  debunking, 73, 173
  experiencing, 166
  misleading, 7
  negative/"loud" American, 78, 182
  "overly friendly" Americans, 81
  unawareness of, 39
Strangers, communicating with, 134
Street crossing, 113
Student aid resources, 216. *See also*
  Expenses and funding
Student discounts, 108, 118
Study abroad offices, 53
Studying. *See* Classroom experience
Switzerland, 78, 96

T
Table manners, 66, 124
Taxi service, 114, 151, 156
Telephone
  cell phones with international calling
    plans, 37
  international phone cards, 34, 199
  Internet phone service, 35
Television, 171
Tetanus, 27
Thailand, 80, 123, 124, 136
Time
  management, 92
  sense of, 68, 112, 122
Tipping, 125
Tokyo, Japan, 8
Tonal languages, 58
Touching, 155
Translation
  in classroom, 104
  tools, 63, 103, 201
Transportation, public, 67, 69
Travel dictionary, 114
Travel guides, 53, 158, 213
Travel insurance, 159
Travel resources, 215
Tutors, 103
Typhoid fever, 26

U
Uganda, 183
Ukraine, 70, 153, 193
United Kingdom, 80. *See also* England;
  Scotland
United States
  see also Ambassadorship
  culture, 170
  embassies, 156
  policies, 165
  State Department, 25, 156
Uruguay, 91

V
Vaccinations, 27
Values, 39
Vegetarian/vegan diets, 125
Ventin, James, 13
Vienna, Austria, 122
Vietnam, 91
Villa Grimaldi, 195
Visas, 19-20
Visits, from family, 36, 199
Voice-over IP technology, 35
Volunteer(ing), 144–46
  resources, 210–11
  sample opportunities, 146

W
Walking, speed of, 78
Waving, 80
Weather, 113
Webcams, 36
Weekend excursions, 128–29. *See also*
  Exploring
Whistles, 159
Wine, 123
Work and teach resources, 212
Working options, 52

Z
Zakharov, Dmitriy, 65, 70, 122, 142, 153,
  193

224   ✺   Index